SOCIAL SURVEY
METHODS

A Fieldguide for Development Workers

Development Guidelines, No. 6
(Series Editor: Brian Pratt)

Paul Nichols

First published by Oxfam 1991

Reprinted by Oxfam GB 1998

© Oxfam 1991

ISBN 0 85598 126 1

A catalogue record for this publication is available from the British Library.

Available from the following agents:
for the USA: Stylus Publishing LLC, PO Box 605, Herndon, VA 20172-0605
tel 800 232 0223; fax 703 661 1501; email styluspub@aol.com
for Canada: Fernwood Books Ltd., PO Box 9409, Stn. A, Halifax, Nova Scotia B3K 5S3
tel 902 422 3302; fax 902 422 3179; email fernwood@istar.ca
for southern Africa: David Philip Publishers, PO Box 23408, Claremont,
Cape Town 7735, South Africa
tel. +27 (0)21 64 4136; fax +27 (0)21 64 3358; email dpp@iafrica.com
for Australia: Bushbooks, PO Box 1958, Gosford, NSW 2250
tel. 02 4323 3274; fax 02 9212 2468; email bushbook@ozemail.com.au

For the rest of the world, contact Oxfam Publishing, 274 Banbury Road,
Oxford OX2 7DZ, UK.
tel + 44 (0)1865 311311; fax + 44 (0)1865 313925; email publish@oxfam.org.uk

Published by Oxfam GB
274 Banbury Road, Oxford OX2 7DZ, UK
(registered as a charity, no. 202918)

Designed and typeset by Oxfam Design Department JM 637 Dec 90
Printed by Oxfam Print Unit

Oxfam GB is a member of Oxfam International.

CONTENTS

FOREWORD

The increased sophistication of non-governmental organisation (NGO) relief and development programmes has led to a demand for improved information about the people with whom NGOs work; their needs, relationships and problems. The scale of NGO activity means that it is no longer possible to rely on the perceptions and knowledge of a single individual to inform the choice of action and project design.

To meet the requests for guidance from fieldworkers wishing to carry out various types of data collection and analysis which will provide them with accurate and relevant information, Oxfam is producing two complementary books. The present volume is the first of these; it is a practical guide to social survey methodologies designed to help fieldworkers decide when and how to conduct a survey. The second volume (*Data collection for Fieldworkers* by Brian Pratt) is a more general guide to all aspects of data collection, including for whom and why information is required, and the data needed for project design, appraisal, monitoring and evaluation. It introduces the range of approaches open to development workers, indicating when and where the different methods of information gathering might be appropriate.

As Paul Nichols, the author of this book, indicates, development workers must be wary of too precipitously embarking on a social survey. Surveys can be expensive and time consuming and still not provide adequate answers to the questions being posed. It is important to have a clear idea of exactly what information is required and why, and how accurate it needs to be, before deciding to carry out a social survey. As the book points out, there are less expensive and faster ways of getting information.

This manual is a technical guide to a set of technical approaches and only indirectly touches on wider questions about the use of information, gender bias, alternative community-based approaches to needs assessment and so forth. These important issues are covered in other publications in the Development Guidelines series and fully discussed in the companion volume, *Data Collection for Fieldworkers*.

If social surveys are carried out well they should assist us in understanding gender relations better. Unfortunately, in an imperfect world, gender blindness and biases often enter social surveys and, indeed, other development work. Throughout this book we have tried to highlight where such biases can most likely affect or even negate the survey findings. It is essential to be ever vigilant in order to ensure that existing biases and prejudices are not reinforced and maintained. One of the aims of social surveys must be to question prejudice and seek to establish quantifiable social facts.

Paul Nichols first wrote this book for use in Southern Sudan, so it has been extensively 'field tested' in Sudan, and also in Kenya and Zimbabwe. We are confident, in the light of this, that it will prove extremely helpful for fieldworkers elsewhere. Dr Alan Stanton assisted Paul Nichols by adding some new material and updating and reordering the text in order to make it more useful to a wider readership.

Brian Pratt
Oxfam, Oxford
September 1990.

ACKNOWLEDGEMENTS

Special thanks to: The Public Works and Municipal Congress and Exhibition Council, The Richard Newitt Fund, Voluntary Service Overseas, and The University of Southampton (Department of Social Statistics), who funded and supported the production of the original manual on which this book is based.

Thanks, also, to the many individuals and organisations who gave time to discuss their own research methods or to comment on the draft, especially: The Low Income Housing Unit, South Sudan; The Community Development Support Unit, South Sudan; The Division of Statistics, South Sudan; The Schools Nutrition Unit, South Sudan; The Equatoria Region Agricultural Project, South Sudan; The UNICEF/ILO team in South Sudan (Project No. SUD/79/P06); UNICEF in South Sudan; Mazingira Institute, Nairobi; The Kenya Central Statistical Office; Housing Research and Development Unit, University of Nairobi; Institute of Development Studies, University of Nairobi; Martin Bulmer at the London School of Economics; and Philip Cooper at the University of Southampton. Any errors in the manual are, of course, my own.

The fieldwork and research on which this manual is based were made possible through the personal help of Philip Cooper, Graham Boyd, Joanne Coffey, David Reid, and the VSO field staff in Juba.

Thanks to Dr Alan Stanton for his detailed and painstaking work in checking, adding to and editing this revised version of the text. I would also like to thank Randy Wilson for advice on microcomputers and Vanessa Tilstone for her help in the final stages of the production of the book.

INTRODUCTION

This manual is intended as a guide to social survey and other research methods for development workers. It outlines simple, low-cost techniques for collecting social and economic information in project areas.

The manual is aimed at readers with no specialist knowledge of social research methods or statistics. In particular it is designed to help the rural worker, in more remote areas, on a low budget with little technical back-up.

The plan of the book goes through the practical steps you need to take in carrying out a research project, from initial planning to final presentation of the results.

In Chapter One, Surveys and other social research methods, we introduce the best known available methods, pointing out the advantages and disadvantages of each. Chapter Two, Study design, deals with the practical side of designing a research study, including drawing up a programme and timetable, developing a research outline, and budgeting to get the best results with the resources available. In Chapter Three the focus is on the fieldwork team, including recruitment, training and supervision of fieldworkers. Chapter Four, on form design, looks in detail at how to collect and record information during fieldwork and the various form designs suitable for interview surveys and observational studies. Chapter Five, Choosing the sample, will help you to decide exactly who, or what, to include in the study. It explains the various random and non-random methods for sampling, and how you can choose a sample which accurately represents the area of study in which you are interested. In Chapter Six, Techniques for data analysis, we introduce the simple and straightforward mathematical tools you will need to use to analyse your survey data. It is not assumed that you will always have a computer available — though if you have, so much the better. Chapter Seven goes through the steps involved in processing and analysing the information collected during fieldwork. This involves using the statistical tools outlined in Chapter Six. The final chapter, Chapter Eight, Presenting the findings, deals with communicating the results of your research. As well as preparing reports, it covers a wide range of methods for communicating with different audiences — officials, technical staff, community groups and politicians. The book ends with a glossary of unfamiliar or technical terms and there is an extensive bibliography.

1 SURVEYS AND OTHER SOCIAL RESEARCH METHODS

'You people do so many surveys, but when do we ever see any action?' It is a question which development workers expect to hear, as well as one they ask of themselves. And it is a vital question at the beginning of a handbook centring on this research tool — the best known method of social research.

In this book we will be looking mainly at structured interview surveys which use specially designed forms to collect a standard set of information from a community or area. As project planners, we often need a systematic way of gathering factual data on, for example, age, sex or household size in a given population. We also want to know, again in a systematic and rigorous way, how people live. This can include vital questions on such things as income distribution or water use. Other major issues will be people's beliefs, opinions, and attitudes.

In many cases a survey can be an essential tool. But sometimes it won't be appropriate — which is where we come back to our questioner's doubts at the beginning. In fact, survey experts themselves are the first to warn against any rush to design a questionnaire, or seeing the resulting tables of numbers as the automatic solution to any and every problem. Even when a survey is useful, it is often best used together with other complementary research tools.

Research methods for community needs

Development work depends on an effective partnership between project planners and the local community. Planners cannot rely solely on standard technical solutions, and projects work best when they are in tune with real community needs. Further details of community-based approaches to research can be found in Pratt (forthcoming) and Feuerstein (1986).

It follows that, in addition to the more straightforward data, we need social research to help in shaping projects to fit the community's own view of its needs. As part of project design, planners should try to see a problem from the participants' viewpoints. We must also find out about community resources. What are the strengths of local people? For example, what skills and abilities are under-used? How far could people contribute cash, labour, or supervision and management skills towards self-help solutions?

As well as collecting such descriptive data, we need evaluative tools. We need to look at existing methods and practices, perhaps to develop and improve on them. And once a particular project is under way, we may need to collect information to monitor the programme and review its effectiveness. Is it meeting its targets? Is it satisfying its 'customers'? Social research can tackle such questions in a number of ways. This chapter gives an overview of the main research methods for the development worker to consider, either alongside a social survey or as alternatives to it.

We will begin with what are usually called informal social research methods: participant observation; case studies; the use of key informants; group discussions; and individual in-depth interviews. Then we will mention some more formal methods. As well as surveys, these include studies based on observation of behaviour, and controlled experiments.

Participant observation

Participant observation is a highly effective method of in-depth study in a small community. It usually involves living in the community under study for a period of weeks or months. The researcher participates as fully as possible in community life, keeping detailed notes of what they hear, see and feel about the subjects under study. This approach combines observation, discussion and informal interview. Its effectiveness depends both on gaining acceptance in the community and on careful recording. For example, when studying a housing project in the Sudan, by living in the area a community development worker gained a good understanding of issues such as residents' problems in organising self-help development of their plots; their ability to repay loans; and their difficulties with small building contractors.

A participant observer taps a continuous flow of information. This may prove more valuable to project management than information from a whole series of structured interview surveys, which are more like 'snapshots' and may only show the surface reality.

Case studies

A case study looks in depth at a 'typical case'. In a study of water problems, for example, you might look at just one village. A detailed understanding of infant health care may come from research with a few families. Though a case-study won't give generalised statistical data, it can provide valuable insights. A skilled researcher, who encourages people to talk, can reveal a rich and lively picture.

Key informants

It is often possible to collect valuable information from a few members of the community who are particularly knowledgeable about certain matters. Examples include community leaders, health workers, school teachers and extension officers. Key informants are most reliable on factual matters, such as the services and facilities available to the community. Their opinions and evaluations are also helpful, but for a wider view you need to follow up with a survey or other research project.

Individual in-depth interviews

Individual in-depth interviews differ from those with key informants in that their scope is usually far wider and they are more open-ended. In an unstructured interview, the person interviewed is free to voice their own concerns, and to share in directing the flow of the conversation. The interviewer relies on open questions to introduce topics of interest. The aim is, literally, an 'inter-view': a mutual exploration of the issues, without the researcher imposing his or her ideas. In a semi-structured interview, the researcher has a prepared list of topics — though still not a set list of questions. Interviewers deal with the topics in any order, and phrase questions as they think best in the circumstances.

In-depth interviews are a valuable tool in themselves. They are also an essential exploratory stage in designing a large, structured interview survey. The researcher discovers not only the themes and topics which interviewees see as important, but how they think about and describe them. Building carefully on this preliminary work results in clearer and sharper research questions. For example, in an exploratory health survey you might ask: 'What are the different kinds of illnesses that babies and children under five experience in this village?' The interviewer writes down any illnesses that are mentioned, then asks: 'Are there any others?' In this way it is possible not only to find out which are the most common illnesses, but also to build up a picture of how illnesses are described in the community and which medical terms are understood.

Individual unstructured or semi-structured interviews are especially suitable for work on attitudes or opinions and for dealing with sensitive topics. Aim for a small sample of about thirty people in exploratory interview surveys. But choose your sample carefully. It is important to include a wide range of community opinion.

Group discussions

In group discussions (sometimes called 'focused groups') the interviewer guides a conversation among a small group of six to ten members of the community of interest. These are 'semi-structured', since the interviewer's skills are used to introduce a list of topics, to encourage wide discussion and to learn about the concerns and opinions of community members. What fresh topics will they raise? And what are their priorities?

You should hold several group discussions to make sure of including a wide range of community opinion. It is usually advisable to arrange for members of a group to be of the same sex and to ensure that they share a similar background. The aim is to have them feeling at ease with one another and free to state their views openly. Such discussions are useful in themselves and, like individual interviews, valuable when planning more formal research.

We will now look at formal social research methods.

Controlled observation and experiments

Sometimes the best way of finding out something is simply to go and look. You can use structured forms for systematic recording of observable data. Examples might be latrine types, borehole conditions, or building materials. Controlled observation can be part of a larger study and can also lend itself to carefully designed experiments. Suppose you want to compare the reliability of two new types of hand-pump. Are the observed differences due to real differences between the pumps? Or to other factors such as frequency of use? You can design an experiment where both pumps are tested in the same community, over boreholes of similar depth, each having the same system of supervision and maintenance. Repeating the experiment in more than one community increases the reliability of your results. In a similar way, you could compare different crop varieties, loan schemes or health care projects, studying their effectiveness over a period of time.

Such experiments are often expensive and time-consuming. For planning at the local level, you may have to rely on a less systematic comparison of informed opinion. However, for large-scale decisions affecting major programmes, the time and effort invested in a carefully designed experiment involving observation and recording of data may be repaid many times over.

Social surveys

As we have said, social surveys use specially designed interview forms. In a large structured survey, the range of possible answers to each question is known in advance and often listed on the form, so that the interviewer simply marks the appropriate reply. If the range of answers is not known, the study designer conducts a pre-test or pilot survey to test the questions and see what answers are given. When the community of interest is small (say, less than 200 households) you may perform a complete (100 per cent) survey. In larger communities and in urban areas you will have to choose a sample of households for interview. All types of people in the community must be properly represented.

In order to design a good structured interview survey, you need a full knowledge of the problem you are studying. This in itself limits their use. When you are working in a new area, or planning a new kind of development project, you will often need methods which are more suitable for exploratory study.

Choosing a research strategy

The choice of a research strategy depends on the purpose of the research, looking broadly at the kind of questions to be explored. The aim is to move from some general ideas on information requirements to a set of detailed objectives and specific questions to which answers are urgently needed.

There are no strict rules for the choice of methods. Generally, you need to strike a balance between the money and time available, and the depth and breadth of the information needed. Formal methods work best when you want more precise, statistical answers to carefully defined questions on topics which are thoroughly understood; they are powerful tools for collecting a broad range of standard information on a large population. Statistical methods give precise estimates and you can assess their reliability. This gives support to your findings and interpretation.

Informal methods are often chosen when time and money are short. They give a rapid 'feel' for a problem. But they are also essential in exploring community attitudes and priorities and when dealing with sensitive topics in depth. They can give a rich understanding of community life, and help to set up a dialogue between planners and the community.

This means that, even when a development project has clear information needs, a mixture of research methods should be used where possible to allow cross-checking of information collected in different ways. A structured, formal research programme will be most effective when it builds on the insights and understanding gained from previous informal work. Participant observation or in-depth individual interviews are powerful tools for learning from local people, and also for enabling them to be actively involved in shaping the research questions.

For these reasons, major research projects using large-scale structured interview surveys usually begin with a period of open-ended exploratory work using the informal methods mentioned. Such methods may also be used in following up a survey, as ways of looking at difficult topics in more detail.

Sometimes it is useful to use structured methods to open a relationship which you will develop later using informal methods. A participant observer, on first arriving in a community, may begin with some small-scale structured interviewing work to collect basic facts. Once trust has been established, the atmosphere is more suitable for informal work.

Here is a brief example, illustrating the choice of methods or combination of methods. Let's suppose we need information on employment — a central part of the simplest economic profile. And let's say that, in a rural area, we are looking at patterns of employment in a farming community. Some of the main factors are probably:

• The use of labour (paid or unpaid) of different age groups, including women and children.

• How labour is organised, including hired labour and workgroups.

• Production at both village and household levels.

• Home consumption, trading and sale of produce.

To get a general picture, we could organise periods of participant-observation and interviews with key-informants. This initial research is important, particularly in collecting meaningful data on informal work. For more detailed information we can design in-depth case-studies of particular types of informal workers. More exact data may need a carefully-timed, single survey to interview farmers and other village workers. With extra resources and time, we can arrange regular, repeated surveys, probably with a panel in several villages (a panel is a small sample for repeat visits). Alternatively, a well-resourced research project can organise observation surveys, recording the activities of all workers on a sample of farms over the study period. This method is accurate, but time-consuming and expensive.

When do we see any action?

This book concentrates on research that does lead primarily to action. Such a general approach is often called 'Action Research'. This is not a separate method, but a commitment to learning about and dealing with real problems in a concrete situation. The aim is to feed back what researchers find out so that agency staff or local people can then make immediate changes and adjustments to their projects and plans.

In recent years, rural development workers have successfully developed a research method called Rapid Rural Appraisal (RRA). Again, this approach seeks answers to practical problems. However, as the name suggests, Rapid Rural Appraisal aims to do this quickly, flexibly and cheaply. A multi-disciplinary team of experts will spend one or two weeks learning from local people about the key problems of an area. The aim is to get sufficient knowledge, without too much unnecessary detail, in order to identify priorities and offer general practical proposals. Rapid Rural Appraisal deliberately uses several different methods of gathering information as a way of cross-checking and building up a picture of a local situation. It can include direct observation, semi-structured interviews, the use of key informants and group discussions and workshops. Rapid Rural Appraisal will avoid formal survey questionnaires, large samples, and statistical analysis, because they are time-consuming and costly. But it will make full use of existing written material, including any previous surveys.

SUMMARY

Choose social research methods according to the information you need. Usually, this will involve using a mixture of methods. Consider informal methods for looking at topics in depth, to explore community attitudes and priorities and to deal with sensitive topics. Use formal methods when you need precise statistical information on well-defined topics. Cross-check information collected in different ways. Try to keep an open mind, especially in the early stages of any research.

One last point: always think carefully about your particular situation and research questions. Be cautious; even where a combination of methods have been used successfully before, it is a good idea to learn by doing pre-tests yourself. Adapt and modify the methods used to fit your own needs.

2 STUDY DESIGN

This chapter takes us into the practical side of designing a research study. The aim of good study design and management is to get the best results possible with the limited resources available. A realistic programme enables you to control and manage the study effectively and to produce the results when they are needed. We will assume that the principal research tool chosen is a social survey. But most of the issues covered in this chapter apply to other kinds of research, too.

Programme and timetable

Before finally selecting a research strategy, always work out a detailed study programme, with a timetable and budget. The best way to begin is to make a careful checklist of tasks to be completed. The list below shows the likely sequence of tasks involved in running a social survey. (Don't worry if some of the terms listed here are unfamiliar. We will come to them later in the book.) You can refer back to the checklist to see how each topic fits into the programme.

PLANNING AND DESIGN

- Discussion and information review.

- Preparing a short paper listing research questions.

- Comparing alternative research strategies.

- Preparing a study programme and budget.

- Obtaining official permissions.

- Mapping or listing target population (preparing the sampling frame).

- Drafting form(s).

- Drafting a tabulation plan.

- Initial discussion and modification of draft form.

- Field testing of draft form and working procedures (the pre-test).

- Preparing the final form.

- Typing and printing the form and training materials.

- Planning the staff training programme.

FIELDWORK

- Assembling the fieldwork team.

- Staff training.

- Completing the fieldwork.

- Supervision of fieldworkers.

- Checking and filing returned forms.

DATA ANALYSIS

- Staff training.

- Checking forms. Editing and coding work.

- Transferring data to summary data sheets or to computer.

•Preparing data tables.

•Calculating summary statistics, preparing charts and graphs, other data analysis.

•Studying tables and drawing conclusions from the data.

PRESENTING FINDINGS

•Planning the report.

•Drafting the report.

•Discussing and finalising the report.

•Printing and distributing the report and any summaries or pamphlets.

•Organising seminars, workshops, and discussions with project managers.

•Public and media presentations.

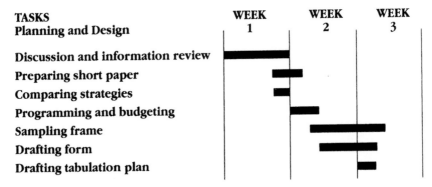

TASKS Planning and Design	WEEK 1	WEEK 2	WEEK 3
Discussion and information review			
Preparing short paper			
Comparing strategies			
Programming and budgeting			
Sampling frame			
Drafting form			
Drafting tabulation plan			

Using your checklist, work out a timetable. One useful technique is to lay out the programme in the form of a table showing the sequence of tasks and allocating a time-span to each task (some will overlap).

For a study proposal, you may want to include a summary programme, which can be shown something like this

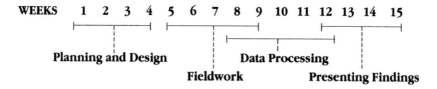

WEEKS   1   2   3   4   5   6   7   8   9   10   11   12   13   14   15

Planning and Design   Data Processing

Fieldwork   Presenting Findings

Information review and discussion

In Chapter One, we said that our research should try to provide answers to urgent questions. A vital preliminary task is to find out and review what is already known about the general research questions. This begins with 'desk research' — making full use of earlier written work. Avoid duplication; it is a waste of time, effort, and scarce resources. Perhaps this seems obvious; unfortunately, only too frequently, just as a new research report is completed, a useful earlier report is discovered tucked away in a cupboard! So review all available, relevant information. Check departmental files. Are there any technical references in books and journals, or data from previous surveys on related topics? Are you in touch with other places with a similar problem?

Discuss the problem area as widely as possible, both formally and informally. Contact the relevant officials in government and non-governmental organisations (NGOs). Speak to elected community representatives, community groups and other key informants. As you collect background material, file it carefully. Open files on each major research topic to store extra notes, references and pieces of analysis as you go along.

It is useful to set up a database indexing all sources of information. A database is like a library card-indexing system; the user looks up the topic or area of interest and obtains details of all data sources available. Databases are often computerised, but a card-index may suit your purposes just as well. A well-maintained database is a valuable resource to both project planners and researchers. A system of this type saves weeks of work, and helps to make the fullest possible use of existing data. It is essential if agencies and units are to share and co-ordinate resources. This sort of sharing is a basic need, not a luxury.

Preparing a research outline

You are now in a position to write a short paper outlining the problem area, discussing previous attempts to solve the problem and listing clear research questions which need to be answered. When you are identifying research questions, concentrate on what is really important for project design purposes. Test research ideas by asking yourself: 'Exactly how will this information help to improve project design?'

To develop a research strategy from the list of research questions you will have to think carefully about the issues considered in Chapter One. What information do you need? What mix of formal and informal methods will work best in finding it out?

In Chapter One, we used the example of employment patterns. Suppose, now, you are studying income levels. You will not be in a position to design a formal structured survey without understanding some basic issues. Perhaps some informal work is needed to settle the following questions:

- How important is cash income to the well-being of the household?

- What are the main formal and informal sources of cash income?

- Do many households either support or receive support from members living elsewhere?

- If food or livestock production are important, how can they be measured?

Ask yourself how precise the information must be. Is a rough estimate good enough, or is it important to measure small changes? A further issue is whether you can answer the questions by observation, or if you will need to conduct personal interviews. The most accurate way to measure farm yields, for example, is usually to measure field areas and then take crop cut samples from several fields. Interviewing the farmer is both quicker and cheaper, but will the estimates be reliable enough for your purposes? There are also questions of timescale. Will a single, one-off 'snapshot' answer the question, or is repeated data collection needed (such as a 'before and after' study)? If you are interested in changes taking place over a period of time, you will need to decide between carrying out repeated social surveys and using 'continuous' research methods, such as participant observation.

Finally, there is a question we will look at in more detail in later chapters: do you need to collect a cross-section of views from the whole community or can you focus on particular groups? What exactly is the target population?

Budgeting

Preparing a study programme is a good basis for estimating the budget — and if necessary, trimming both. What funds and time are at your disposal? Consider carefully the staff, transport and other resources you will need. The availability of transport obviously determines the area over which the study can take place and therefore the size of sample you can use.

Besides the actual number of staff available, you need to consider their skills and experience. If you plan to use informal methods, fewer fieldworkers will be needed, but they must have a good understanding of the topics investigated and be skilled in prompting and leading discussion. Interviewers to carry out structured social surveys need different skills, but can be fully trained in short, intensive courses. Data-processing staff can also be trained quickly, but some statistical skill is essential for coordinating data analysis for a large, structured interview survey. (We will look at the recruitment and training of fieldworkers in the next chapter.)

Your budget must include all extra, non-routine costs, which are not part of a project's normal running costs. Estimate any special bonuses and field allowances for permanent staff and the cost of hiring temporary fieldworkers or research assistants. Include any extra fuel and maintenance costs, as well as items such as extra stationery and printing. Always add a percentage for 'contingencies' — unexpected delays or problems during fieldwork.

As well as drawing up a cash budget, it is sensible to estimate 'hidden' costs — such as the time permanent staff spend on the study, rather than on their normal tasks. This will help to give a truer costing for the research. Match your study to the time available. Note that data processing (not including report writing) is likely to take at least as long as the fieldwork. Make sure you have plenty of time to prepare findings and conclusions and to discuss results with project managers. There is no point in collecting data which remains unused and becomes out-of-date because of a lack of resources to analyse and disseminate it.

SUMMARY

If social research is to be useful and cost-effective, careful planning is essential. Work out a timetable and a list of tasks to be carried out. A well-maintained database, giving the source of existing relevant information, is essential. Having drawn up an outline programme, estimate all the costs and make sure the resources of time, staff and money available to you are adequate for the proposed research.

3 THE FIELDWORK TEAM

Except for the smallest survey project, you will need to assemble and train a fieldwork team. Good fieldworkers are vital if the research is to win co-operation from the community.

Recruitment

Who makes a good fieldworker? Personality is important; they should be open and friendly people, yet polite and sensitive enough to encourage honest, sometimes intimate conversation. Personal appearance — including dress and demeanour — gives subtle (and maybe not so subtle) signals. As fieldwork is often done alone, it requires both an ability to get on with the job, and the initiative to report problems as they arise. Conditions are often hard and fieldworkers may have to spend time away from home. Choose people who are well-motivated and enthusiastic about the research and convinced of its value.

A good basic education is usually (though not always) needed. Staff working with interview schedules and survey forms must be literate, and comfortable with numbers and basic arithmetic. Even highly structured forms require more than just neat, careful recording — though this is, of course, essential. Clear, intelligent thinking is needed to ensure that the correct questions are asked and that confused and contradictory answers are sorted out during the interview.

Matching fieldworkers to the community

Select fieldworkers to match the people they will be interviewing. Important factors to be considered include gender, social class and status, and level of education. As a general rule, fieldworkers should be the same sex as interviewees.

For rural areas, local interviewers are normally the best choice. They are fluent in the language or dialect, and usually minimise suspicion and mistrust. Local people can play a valuable part in project design and evaluation, and they will be key informants on some aspects of the community.

If you employ local people with only basic literacy skills, they may require training (perhaps weekly classes over some months) to develop their writing skills and basic arithmetic, as well as to learn fieldwork methods. The advantage is that these fieldworkers will be very closely matched with the people they will be interviewing, and likely to be able to deal with sensitive or intimate topics. As well as the benefit to local people of gaining skills and understanding, an investment in training is especially valuable for long-term studies involving repeated surveys. However, there are circumstances in which people find it difficult to talk to someone from their immediate community. Then it may be better if fieldworkers come from neighbouring villages.

Another effective approach is to second staff already working in a related job. So, for a short period, a team of environmental health workers might conduct a sanitation survey, or agricultural extension officers could undertake an agricultural study. You need to negotiate secondments well in advance with the appropriate agencies, and plan the fieldwork to meet their requirements. Using existing staff has major advantages. Trained, experienced staff are practised in gaining the trust of people they interview. They have few problems with the more technical aspects of a survey. At the same time, they gain experience in social research and add to their understanding of community problems related to their usual work. They may have much to offer towards possible solutions to the problems identified. And, of course, they continue to work in the community after the study is complete. If the same group of workers is seconded regularly, they can develop their fieldwork skills over a longer period.

A similar solution is to hire or arrange for the secondment of people such as school teachers or community development workers, already living close to the study area. They need not have specialist knowledge of the problems. Such people, if known and trusted by the community, can complete fieldwork with a minimum of travel and disruption. They are well placed for a participant observation study over a period of time, and for 'before and after' interview surveys and other monitoring work.

A different approach is to employ school-leavers or students. This is often very successful, especially when they have a real interest in social research. But there can sometimes be problems, particularly relating to age and social class. For instance, in some societies young people are not expected to 'cross-question' their elders. If university students are seen as potential members of an 'educated elite' this can result in a loss of trust by the interviewees. Students may find that the repetitive day-to-day routine of survey work does not match their expectations of 'research', and they may become bored and disillusioned.

Training

Every fieldwork team needs training. Experienced fieldworkers can sometimes master a new survey form in a two- or three-day course, but they will usually need longer. For major surveys, using long forms and advanced interview methods, up to three weeks of training and practice may be needed. The training period should include both formal sessions and supervised fieldwork practice interviews.

Remember that a training programme is also an opportunity to test recruits. Make it clear that all fieldworkers must complete a period of probation, and that those not reaching an acceptable standard will not be offered further work. If you include formal tests in the training programme, make sure they do more than just assess whether fieldworkers have memorised training materials. Test their understanding of the aims of the research project and of the research tools being used. It is most important to check their ability to perform realistic practical fieldwork tasks.

Planning a training programme

Introduce the background to the survey. Explain the purpose of the research and the importance of the information which fieldworkers are to collect. Discuss how they will introduce the survey to interviewees. Make certain that fieldworkers have a realistic idea of projects likely to result from the survey, so they avoid raising any false hopes.

Use practical methods as far as possible. Always avoid long lectures. For example, explaining how the sample will be located in the field often involves the use of maps. Hold classroom exercises in map-work, followed by field exercises. It is useful to build translation work into the training programme. Fieldworkers chosen for their ability to understand local languages can translate the survey form, as a way of becoming familiar with the form and thinking carefully about its meaning. (Back-translation — when an outsider retranslates into the original language — will help check the accuracy of a translation.)

Plan the bulk of training time around the interview form, and always have plenty of spare forms available. Before the sessions begin, prepare a detailed manual for using the form. This must include all necessary definitions; instructions for recording answers; how and when to probe; and details of local measurements. The manual can include extra material on choosing people to interview, observation methods and even notes on vehicle maintenance.

Structure your training so that everyone can easily follow each session in the manual. Deal with each section of the form in turn. Give a short introduction, followed by questions, discussion and — most valuable of all — practical exercises. One effective practical method is the mock interview.

Mock interviews

To set up mock interviews, prepare cards (or projection slides) showing profiles of people to be interviewed. Cover the main characteristics you are likely to find in the field, and include all the details necessary for someone to play the part of the person interviewed. Carefully designed standard profiles enable you to check fieldworkers' understanding of the form. The team can be split into pairs, each person taking a turn in the role of interviewer and person interviewed.

Alternatively, two people can be chosen to carry out a mock interview and everyone else can observe them, recording the answers given and then comparing their completed records and discussing any differences. Another idea is for the 'interviewer' to leave the room while the rest of the team construct a profile for the 'person interviewed'. The completed forms should be kept and checked carefully. They can show if definitions are being used correctly, if the right questions are asked in each case, and so on.

Supervised field trials

Follow up classroom interviews with supervised field trials. Again, these are practice interviews, where you are training the interviewers, not pre-testing the survey. A supervisor should observe each fieldworker, discussing the interview with them afterwards and carefully checking the completed form. This is the stage at which fieldworkers can be given most guidance on their interviewing technique, in particular on avoiding bias and encouraging honest and full answers.

An interviewer must appear to be sympathetic, but neutral. They must take care not to reveal their expectations or their own feelings about an issue to the people they are interviewing, so as not to influence the kind of answers they are given. Supervisors should draw attention to comments or gestures which could signal the interviewer's agreement or disagreement with an answer. Is the interviewer an interested, attentive listener? Are they sensitive to resistance to the interview or to certain questions, possibly affecting the reliability of the answers given?

Fieldworker supervision and management

Careful supervision and management are vital, both to keep fieldwork running smoothly and to ensure you collect good quality data. Before any data are collected, design record systems to keep track of all information coming in. For example, set up a system to record when interview forms are: (i) with fieldworkers, (ii) returned, (iii) checked, and (iv) processed. This system enables you to keep track of the completed forms, ensures forms do not get lost and speeds up data processing.

Make sure you obtain all the correct permissions before fieldwork begins. In most countries the Central Statistical Office must approve all social survey work. You will also need to discuss the study with local leaders in advance of the fieldwork, explaining why the information is needed. In rural areas, the manual for fieldworkers can include instructions for entering new villages. List the order in which local leaders are to be approached, prepare letters of introduction and outline standard project introductions.

Supervision

Except for the smallest projects, you need one or more experienced fieldworkers as supervisors. Hire them in the early stage of the training programme. They need special training in supervision work and a particularly full understanding of the purpose of the study.

Supervisors may be separate appointments, or a senior fieldworker could spend part of the week visiting other members of the team. In a small urban study, or where a fieldwork team travels together, a single supervisor may be sufficient. A larger rural study requires a supervisor in each area. There must be enough supervisors to check every fieldworker's work at least two or three times a week and preferably every day.

The central task of the supervisor is checking completed forms. Everyone can make mistakes, especially at first. Typical problems include incorrectly missing out questions, or recording inconsistent answers, contradicted by an answer elsewhere on the form. Sometimes the fieldworker or the person being interviewed has not understood the question. Any answers which sound unlikely should be checked. Apart from obvious errors on individual forms, supervisors should discuss with each fieldworker the reliability of each question and any specific problems. Fieldworkers usually sense some resistance on the part of an interviewee or an inability to give an accurate answer.

Supervisors should compare the work of all fieldworkers. Is one of them imposing her or his own style on responses? If response rates diverge widely, supervisors should try to find out why particular fieldworkers record a high number of refusals or non-contacts. Supervisors may need to carry out some repeat interviews.

Decide and clarify the supervisors' general responsibilities. Normally, you will expect them both to deal with practical day-to-day problems during fieldwork and to keep in regular contact with survey headquarters. In addition, they should be asked to prepare a short report on field problems and interview conditions, after discussion with fieldworkers.

Some general points

Fieldworker morale is important. Terms and conditions must reflect any difficult working conditions. For both fieldworkers and supervisors, make sure that the rates of pay are about the same as those used by other agencies for the same sort of work.

Consider whether to use single interviewers, pairs or large teams. Pairs of interviewers are often very effective; for example, a male and female pair can interview husband and wife at the same time and, where the study involves both observation and interview, one person can carry out observation work while the other completes an interview. If single interviewers are used, make sure they have regular contact with other team members to compare notes and to keep morale high.

You also need to think carefully about the best interview location. The interviewee's home is convenient in many ways, but it can be hard to find privacy. For some studies, interviews in the workplace (perhaps a farmer's field) are more useful. Encourage fieldworkers to be aware of interview conditions. When conditions are not good — for example, when a crowd begins to gather — the fieldworker should make an appointment to come back later. Design forms with space for comment on interview conditions where the fieldworker notes if respondents seem bored or distracted, or if interruptions disturb the flow of the interview. Fieldworkers can keep a diary, noting particular problems for discussion with supervisors during fieldwork.

This raises the question of how to treat unusual answers, particularly where the interview has been, for some reason, unsatisfactory. One particular interview may produce 'extreme' values for some data, far outside the general set of values. If the interviewee is judged to be totally unreliable, it is better to discard the results of that interview rather than distort the final presentation of the data from the survey. But if it is not possible to make firm judgements about the validity of the results obtained, it is advisable to record the extreme values in the findings but to add a note in your presentation about the particular circumstances of the interview which produced these values.

Hold a debriefing session for the complete team at the end of the fieldwork. Work through each part of the form in turn. Discuss any problems with the wording of questions, failures to answer or possible misunderstandings.

SUMMARY
It is essential to put time and effort into recruiting good fieldworkers, and training them thoroughly. Training should use practical exercises where possible. Fieldworkers must understand the purpose of the research, how to locate the sample, and how to use the form, and be given guidance on interview technique.

Supervisors should be trained to deal with practical fieldwork problems. They should monitor the daily progress of fieldworkers and keep in contact with headquarters. They should also tell you about fieldworker morale.

Encourage fieldworkers to record interview conditions, and to discuss problems with supervisors as they arise and at a final debriefing session for the whole team.

4 FORM DESIGN

A form is a document used to record data during fieldwork. The aim is to collect sets of standardised information, in a uniform way. Each form needs careful preparation if it is to suit the purposes and conditions of the research.

Types of form include:

- A sheet recording a standard set of observations.

- A checklist of information to be collected.

- An exact list of questions for a personal interview.

The third type — often called a questionnaire, or interview schedule — is used for structured, formal interviews. We will concentrate on this, as it is the most difficult to design.

In Chapter One we described how preliminary work is used to develop a set of detailed research questions. These questions are the starting point for form design. Remember that you only want to collect information which is essential to answer your research questions. You will need to think about the information you need to record in the field, the way it will be analysed and the way it will help to answer the study questions.

We will begin by looking at different ways of collecting factual data. This will be followed by a discussion about recording people's beliefs and attitudes. The chapter ends by looking at form layout and how to make the document a clear and helpful tool.

Collecting factual data from observation

Some of the more descriptive factual information (often called 'hard data') can be collected by direct observation. To record observations, design a form setting out clear details on how to classify each observed variable. It is essential to give exact instructions to the fieldworker. In the following example, fieldworkers studying household water supply were asked to record explicit information on the age and gender of people collecting water; the containers they used; the quantity of water collected by each user; time spent at the source by each user; other activities, such as washing clothes, at the source; periods when water was not available; and the size of the queue.

HOUSEHOLD WATER SUPPLY STUDY : USER OBSERVATION SHEET

Observer No._____   Sheet No._____   From: _____

To: _____

Queue size
at start time _____

Periods water
not available

1 from: _____ to: _____

2 from:_____ to: _____

3 from:_____ to: _____

USER Number. Ring if Interviewed	SEX M/F	AGE 5-9 10-14 15>	CONTAINER Gerrycan;Tin;Other		ARRIVAL TIME	DEPARTURE TIME	ADDITIONAL ACTIVITIES AT SOURCE
			1	2			

Design your form to assist both fieldworkers and the staff who will code the data later. In the example above, most column headings list a limited range of possible answers. These are called 'closed' questions. Use closed questions wherever possible; they are far easier to analyse than open questions. But check that the full range of possible answers is listed and that your classification is useful. Note that the column 'Additional Activities At Source' is an 'open' question, requiring the fieldworker to describe activities other than water collection. There were so many possibilities that no range of answers was given.

When the form above was being designed, it was necessary to find out information about the youngest person likely to collect water and about the different containers in use. Informal discussion provided answers to these questions, but sometimes you will need formal pre-testing to find out the likely range of answers.

Collecting factual data from interviews

When interviewing, you can often record simple facts directly into a carefully prepared table. Tables are useful for straightforward numerical or one-word answers, recording standard information. The example below comes from a survey of water sellers:

Daily Operations: FILL IN TABLE

	No.vehicles in use daily	No.trips per vehicle daily	Units in which water is sold	Sale price(s) per unit	Load size(s) (No.of units)
DONKEY CARTS					
LORRIES					

Fieldworkers using a table like this are free to ask for the information as they think best. There is no problem of translation, since there is no need to use a standard set of words for each interview. Only simple facts should be recorded directly into tables. Don't try to use tables for exploring complicated issues or different shades of meaning. For tables, as with observation sheets, use closed questions as far as possible. Only include open questions if the possible answers have just one or two words.

Where there are many possible answers, or each answer is quite long, list the range of possibilities underneath the table:

ACTIVITY	USUAL LOCATION 1 (27—34)	HOW OFTEN 2 (35—42)	AMOUNT USED 3 (43—50)	ENOUGH WATER 4 (51—58)
Cooking/Drinking	□	□	□	□
Brewing	□	□	□	□
Washing pots	□	□	□	□
Bathing 0-4 yrs	□	□	□	□
Bathing 5-14 yrs	□	□	□	□
Bathing 15> yrs	□	□	□	□
Other water uses:	□	□	□	□
- - - - - - - - - - -				
- - - - - - - - - - -	□	□	□	□

(1) Usual location of each activity
CODE IN COL. 1 ↑

On this plot	1	Other	5
At the river	2		
At the khor	3	NA	6
At the public tap	4	DK	7

(2) How often each activity takes place. For bathing, take frequency per person

CODE IN COL. 2 ↑

5+times daily	1	Every 2 to 3 days	6
4 times daily	2	Every 4 to 5 days	7
3 times daily	3	Every 6 to 7 days	8
2 times daily	4	Less than every	9 days
1 time daily	5	Less than every	7 days
	NA		0
	DK		-

Even without a table, if you only want straightforward facts you do not always need to write out questions in full. Instead, you can use key words. In the next example, key words in closed questions are used to collect simple information about water usage.

		Main	Other(1)	Other(2)
	Direct Supply	01	01	01
	Donkey Carrier	02	02	02
Water sources used	Yoke carrier	03	03	03
during past month	Lorry	04	04	04
	Neighbour's tap	05	05	05
RING ONE CODE IN	Public tap	06	06	06
EACH COLUMN	Borewell	07	07	07
	Nile	08	08	08
	Khor	09	09	09
	NA	10	10	10
	DK	11	11	11
	Other _ _ _ _ _ _ _ _ _	12	12	12
	- - - - - - - - - - - - -			

Overall, are you satisfied with your existing water supply?
READ OUT   Very satisfied   1 ——————▶ Go to Q8
            Fairly satisfied   2

36

		1st	2nd	3rd
RING ONE CODE	Not satisfied	3		
	NA	4		
	DK	5		
IF FAIRLY SATISFIED OR NOT SATISFIED RING ONE CODE IN EACH COLUMN ON THE RIGHT				
	Danger to health	1	1	1
	Looks dirty	2	2	2
	Smells bad	3	3	3
	Tastes bad	4	4	4
	Inconvenient	5	5	5
	Expensive	6	6	6
Problems with existing water supply	Cannot get enough	7	7	7
	NA	8	8	8
	DK	9	9	9
	Other _____	0	0	0

For reliable results, the wording of questions must be clear. Clear questions will aid translation. You can sometimes add a translation on the same form without overcrowding it. With fully framed questions you probably need a separate form for the translation.

Recording attitudes

We often need to know about people's attitudes — their opinions, beliefs and feelings. It is harder to collect reliable data on attitudes than on more factual matters. It is vital to treat such topics with caution, studying them carefully and in detail. One approach is to assess attitudes by looking at people's actions. You need to assess to what extent the issues are part of a respondent's personal, daily experience. A woman asked about improving the collection of river water may have more concrete ideas and opinions than, for example, a farmer who, never having seen an extension worker, is asked for his views on the extension service.

It is advisable to explore attitudes through in-depth case studies as well as structured interviews. Even well-designed questionnaires can only scratch the surface of what people really think, but longer informal discussions will fill out the picture. Exploring people's attitudes raises major problems of language and the communication of exact meanings. These difficulties increase when translating from one language to another. You may need to interview in more than one language, especially in urban areas.

We can see how such problems arise when we look at a common method for collecting data on attitudes — the use of scales. Scaling means constructing an ordered list of opinions or attitudes. Respondents select the statement(s) they agree with:

Overall, are you satisfied with your existing water supply?

INTERVIEWER READ OUT	Very satisfied	1
	Fairly satisfied	2
RING ONE CODE	Not satisfied	3
	Don't know	4

This simple scale aims at little more than a head count. Even so, there are pitfalls. To get reliable results it is essential that all respondents understand the scale in the same way. Here, the English word 'satisfied' has different shades of meaning. Other words used in a survey may have more than one meaning. For example, the word 'fair' can mean 'just' as well as 'neither good, nor bad'; 'poor' can mean both 'of low quality' and 'having little money'. In a local language, the best translation of 'satisfied' may differ from the English word. Respondents may answer without using the scale as intended; they could even fail to see the scale as a range of attitudes along a single dimension.

To minimise these problems, try to use words which have only one, clear meaning. If you want to classify 'for and against' as in the example above, pair a word or phrase with its opposite, and add a 'middle-of-the-range' word or phrase between them. Careful translation, back-translation (see the glossary) and pre-testing is essential. Be suspicious if nearly all the answers fall in one category; this often means the scale is not working well.

Stress to interviewers that they must always ask the questions in the same way, keeping to the exact wording. In the example above, if some interviewers miss out the word 'overall', the tone of the question alters. If they change 'satisfied' to something similar (like 'pleased' or 'happy') the responses will change. A number of such small errors taken together can make the question almost useless.

Time scales

To find out about intentions rather than opinions, consider using a time scale. This can help to distinguish between those who have a definite plan to do something, and those with only a vague idea. For example:

When do you think you will next increase the price of your water?

READ OUT	During the next three months	☐
	During the next six months	☐
	During the next year	☐
	After a year	☐
	Other	_____

Answer lists

The answer list is a way of measuring strength of feeling among a standard range of possible answers. Respondents choose which answer(s) they agree with. In the example below, the list is read out in full, before asking for a reply. The fieldworker previously explains this procedure to the person being interviewed:

Which of the following sicknesses do you consider the most important problem for your children?

READ OUT

1. Meningitis	6. Measles	
2. Malaria	7. Sleeping Sickness	
3. Diarrhoea	8. Schistosomiasis	
4. Respiratory Infections	(Bilharzia)	
5. Skin Infections/ Diseases	9. Other (specify) ----------	

Lists of this type make analysis easier, as answers are automatically classified in the same way. Without a list, the sicknesses mentioned would be described in many different ways and levels of detail.

To return to an earlier example; some respondents have expressed dissatisfaction with their water supply. To find out exactly what the problem is, you could direct those particular respondents to an answer list:

Overall, are you satisfied with your existing water supply?

READ OUT			
	...Very satisfied	1 ———▶ Go to Q8	
	...Fairly satisfied	2	
	...Not satisfied	3	
RING ONE CODE	NA	4	
	DK	5	

IF FAIRLY SATISFIED OR NOT SATISFIED RING ONE CODE		1st	2nd	3rd
IN EACH COLUMN ON THE RIGHT	Danger to health	1	1	1
	Looks dirty	2	2	2
	Smells bad	3	3	3
	Tastes bad	4	4	4
	Inconvenient	5	5	5
	Expensive	6	6	6
Problems with existing	Cannot get enough	7	7	7
water supply	NA	8	8	8
	DK	9	9	9
	Other	0	0	0

Lists have their disadvantages. Respondents who do not understand them may answer at random, and may not give their true answer if it is not listed. Even with an 'other' category, items not on the list are less likely to be mentioned.

Lists are most effective when a respondent can read and look back over the items. When a respondent cannot read, so that the list has to be read aloud, they may not consider all the alternatives. They may forget the first items mentioned and give an answer using one of the last few, especially if the list is long. If you have to read out a long list, reverse the order of items for half the people interviewed.

Used with caution, scales and lists can give helpful results when exploring beliefs, attitudes and intentions. They call for skilled interviewers and careful training, especially if the interviewer is to avoid leading the respondent.

Using probes

Probes are a general method for asking the respondent to provide further clarification. For example, suppose after certain answers you want respondents to expand on what they have just said. You should instruct interviewers to then use a probe — a neutral phrase such as 'Is there anything else?' or 'Why is that?' Describe each probe instruction on the form as specifically as possible. (And remember to include examples of probes in the fieldwork manual.)

Open questions

While structured surveys should use closed questions as much as possible, open questions are very useful in exploratory and pre-testing work, when you want to find out and list the full range of possible answers. They are often used with probes, for example:

What are the main problems with your accommodation?

(PROBE: Anything else?)

With a large sample, and when resources are stretched, open questions may pose huge problems. Answers will vary in both length and detail. Instead of analysing them using a standard routine, you must think about and summarise each answer separately.

Form layout

We will now look at some general points about the layout of a structured survey form. Think of the interview as a conversation and, we hope, an interesting one. The form's design should help this conversation to flow naturally, without sudden breaks or changes in direction.

Introducing the survey

Before asking the first question, fieldworkers should give respondents certain basic information. This does not need to be written on the form, and interviewers can be informal, using their own words. But do agree a standard format, including the name of the organisation running the survey, its main area of interest, the purpose of the survey and how the results will be used. On the last point, avoid too much detail. It can easily be taken as clues to the kind of answers you expect. People are often ready to tell interviewers 'what they want to hear'. Always insist that interviewers avoid making any false promises or comments which will raise hopes unfairly. They should not give the impression that some new project is planned, if this is not the case.

Order of questions

Keep the first few questions straightforward and easy to answer. They should relate plainly to the purpose of the survey. At this stage you are trying to establish trust, and to reassure the person you are interviewing. Don't scare them off! It is wise to leave questions about beliefs, attitudes and intentions to the later stages of the interview. Only tackle sensitive or embarrassing subjects if it is really necessary. It helps if you give such subjects a short introduction, explaining why you want the information.

Work from the particular to the general. For example, in a water collection study this question would normally come towards the end:

Overall, are you satisfied with this as a place to collect your water?

This type of final, very general question is often useful. Even with a well-designed questionnaire, it may bring out some fresh and interesting possibility. The person you are interviewing may have just such a comment, given the chance to talk. Leave enough space at the end for the interviewer to write down the answer in full, using the respondent's own words.

Interview length

Even when the research topic demands a long interview, do not expect people to give more than one hour of their time. Allowing for introductions and greetings, the questionnaire itself should normally take no longer than 45 minutes. Long, tiring interviews increase the risk of error. On the other hand, if someone has a great personal interest in the subject they will co-operate for much longer. In-depth case studies can often take more time than structured interviews, without tiring the respondent. But if someone is not convinced that the survey has any practical purpose, their patience will run out faster.

Short interviews have other advantages; the sample size can be increased (or fieldwork time reduced); analysis is simpler, and reports are less complicated. You should make every effort to reduce the subjects covered to those which are really useful and important. If you really do need a wide range of detailed information, you can split the form into separate components. Fieldworkers can then make repeat visits, using one component in each session. If this is not feasible (for example, if respondents are not co-operative), you can use each component with a different sub-sample, chosen at random. This method is only useful with a very large sample.

Form size and presentation

The following conventions help to make forms easy to read and use. If the form has several pages, print it on one side of the paper only. Use upper-case (capital letters) for instructions to fieldworkers. Print questions and answers in upper and lower-case letters. List answers and codes in a consistent way in columns down the right-hand side of the form. Leave plenty of space for written answers and for interviewers to add any field notes.

If the answer is a number, use a template to draw square 'boxes' for entering it. Make sure it is clear what units of measurement you are using. Boxes are also useful for ticking answers in a list. Use arrows to show 'skips' (see below). At the top of each form leave a space for the interviewer's name and a form number. In a random household survey, add a small table for details of each visit, so you can keep track of dates and times of visits and the need for follow-up if the respondent is not seen. For example:

Interviewer: *Nancy X Attc*

1st Call Date:	1/2/82	Time:	9.30 am	Result:	not home
2nd Call Date:	3/2/82	Time:	12.20 pm	Result:	Interviewed
3rd Call Date:		Time:		Result:	

English:		Householder:		
Arabic:	✓	Wife:	✓	Ethnic Group: *kakwa*
Other:		Other:		

Large forms are expensive to produce, heavy to carry in the field and difficult to store. Even so, do not try to reduce the size of forms by crowding questions on the page. Interviewers are far more likely to make errors — missing out a question or misreading instructions — when a form is congested, inconsistent and badly organised. Take the next example:

Respondent Name

    Head of household/_____ Spouse/_____

    Relative/_____ Neighbour/_____

    Male/Female/_____ Years lived in Nbi/_____

    Years lived in this house/_____

    How long expecting to stay: Don't know/_____

    No. of years/_____ Leave soon/_____

    Reasons/_____

Employment

    Head of household's main skill _____

    Other skills _____

    Unskilled/_____

    Working?Full time/_____ Part/_____ Unemployed/_____

    Retired/_____

    Place of work? On/near site/_____

    Town centre/_____ Industrial area/_____

    Outside town/_____

    Travel to work? Walk/_____ Bike/_____ P/car/_____

    Matatu/Bus/_____

Single space typing makes this form look crowded and complicated even before you start reading it. The fieldworker is forced to use small writing, which will cause headaches for the person analysing the information. There are few instructions, though the questions are not self-explanatory. Lists of possible answers are not used. For example, how are the interviewers to classify the head of household's main skill? How much detail must they give? Compare the example overleaf:

How far away is your compound?	0 to $\frac{1}{2}$ km	1
	$\frac{1}{2}$ to 1 km	2
INTERVIEWER TO ESTIMATE	1 to $1\frac{1}{2}$ km	3
	$1\frac{1}{2}$ to 2 km	4
RING ONE CODE	More than 2 km	5
	DK	6
	NA	7

How many times do people from your
household come here to collect water per day:

WRITE IN:TIMES PER DAY ☐
IF LESS THAN ONE TRIP PER DAY, WRITE IN   _ _ _ _ _ _ _ _ _ _ _ _ _ _ _ _ _

At what times of day do you usually	Morning up to 7.30	1
come here to collect water?	7.30 up to 9.00	2
(PROBE: Any others?)	9.00 up to 2.30	3
	2.30 up to 4.00	4
	4.00 up to dark	5
RING ALL THAT APPLY	After dark	6
	DK	7
	NA	8

Three questions now take up half a page, rather than three lines. But each question begins on the left-hand margin, so it is difficult to miss a question out. Interviewers are given clear instructions on the form. All these improvements help to save time and reduce errors in the fieldwork. Data analysis will be easier, too, because closed questions are used and the codes are easily seen and copied.

Codes

Coding means giving a number or letter to each possible answer. Codes are a useful way of summarising large amounts of information. They are essential, even for small samples, when data is to be analysed by computer. If you are using a computer, always check that the programme used will be able to read the types of code you are using.

When interviewers have to enter codes during fieldwork, they must be carefully trained. Write clear instructions on the form, and as far as possible, use the same method for recording answers throughout the form. This will reduce the number of errors.

For large samples, questions with many possible answers, and open questions, you may need to leave coding until later. It becomes a separate stage, to be completed when forms are returned to the office. (See Chapter Seven.) In this case, you will need coding instructions. Each box for entering codes is given a reference number. Using this reference number, codes are transferred to numbered columns on data sheets, or typed directly into a computer. If you look back to the table on water use on page 36, you will see that all the possible answers are listed below the table, and the interviewer is instructed to enter the number for that answer in the appropriate column. Each 'water use' is also given a number at the top of the column; cooking/drinking is 27, brewing 28, etc. When the form is returned, the results will be entered in the appropriate place on a data sheet. If water for cooking/drinking is obtained from the river, the figure 2 from column one on the form will be entered against item 27 on the data sheet.

Skips and filters

Think about the question below. Why is it so muddled?

Do you have a job or business or do you normally work on the farm belonging to the household, but did not work yesterday?

The question aims at finding out who did not work yesterday, but requires this information from two groups only: respondents with a job or business, and respondents who normally work on the farm belonging to the household.

The solution is a skip. To make sure that only members of the two groups of interest are asked the question, the skip instructs the fieldworker to by-pass certain questions when interviewing other groups of people. The skip works like this:

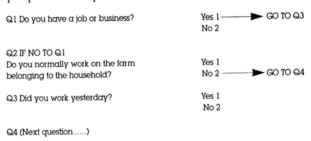

Do everything possible to make skip instructions clear. Check carefully that the skip works as you intend. Work through the form, imagining that you are each possible type of respondent, testing if the form makes sense in every case.

A filter works in much the same way. A group within the target population are 'filtered' through to another part of the form. For example:

Do you have a latrine in this house/compound? YES   NO

IF NO GO TO PAGE 8 ⟶

Dealing with 'awkward' answers

Even with a closed question, using a set list of answers, it is wise to include an 'other' category for answers left out. This is another 'safety net' to catch something which was not met in the pre-test or in previous studies. For an 'other' category, the interviewer should write in the full answer. The category 'not applicable' is useful for showing that the fieldworker did not just forget to ask the question; while a 'don't know' category will often show when an apparently simple question is not being understood correctly.

An example of a structured interview form

To end this chapter, here is an example of a form used in a structured interview survey. It is not presented as an ideal, but simply to demonstrate some of the points made above. The Water Point Survey was carried out by the Regional Ministry of Housing in South Sudan in 1983. The sample was small, so forms were analysed directly, without the use of codes. Note especially the use of: closed questions (with tick boxes (Q.1 and Q.2); key words; tables (Q.3(e), Q.11 and Q.12); skips (Q.2); and clear instructions to fieldworkers.

OPERATOR SURVEY : WATER POINT OPERATORS   WATER POINT REF.NO.

1 Type of water point		2 Respondent		
Kiosk	☐	Licensee/Operator	☐	
Standpipe, no kiosk	☐	Licensee only	☐	
Borewell	☐	Operator,Govt.employee	☐➤	GO TO Q4
Other	☐	Operator,private employee	☐➤	GO TO Q4
		Other	☐➤	GO TO Q4

46

3 ASK IF LICENSEE

a Date license received: _ _ _ _ _ _ _ _ _ _ _ _ _ _ _

b Date license expires: _ _ _ _ _ _ _ _ _ _ _ _ _ _ _

c Last Bill paid: Amount: _ _ _ _ _ _ _ _ _ _ _ _ _ _ _

Period covered: _ _ _ _ _ _ _ _ _ _ _ _ _ _ _

Date paid: _ _ _ _ _ _ _ _ _ _ _ _ _ _ _ _ _

Estimated/Metered: _ _ _ _ _ _ _ _ _ _ _

d Whether other Standpipe/Borewell licenses held:

IF YES, GIVE DETAILS: Number : _ _ _ _ _ _ _ _ _ _ _ _ _ _ _ _ _ _ _

Location : _ _ _ _ _ _ _ _ _ _ _ _ _ _ _ _ _ _ _

e Details of all those helping to operate the water point, including relatives and children

Job	Sex	Age	Relative	Hours per day	Daily pay	Other benefits	Days per week

f Whether written record kept of: Sales: _

Expenditure: _

IF YES, GIVE DETAILS: _

g Do you wish to renew your license when this one expires? _ _ _ _ _ _ _ _ _ _ _ _ _ _ _ _ _ _ _

IF NO, ASK WHY NOT: _

_ _

h Do you have other sources of income apart from this water point? _ _ _ _ _ _ _ _ _ _ _ _ _ _ _ _ _

IF YES, LIST OTHER SOURCES OF INCOME: _

_ _

Which is your main source of income: _

4 a Can the water point be locked? _

IF YES: b Usual opening time: _

c Usual closing time: _

d No. of days open per week: _

5 a Over the past week, has water sometimes not been available during the period the water point was open? _

IF YES: b Usual times not available: _

c Usual reason not available: _

d No. of complete days for which was continuously _ _ _ _ _ _ _ _ _ _ _ _ _ _

not available over the past week? _

6 a Is any record kept of the number of people buying water?

        IF YES: b Describe how records are kept
                     c Numbers collecting over the past week:

7 a Has any maintenance been required over the past month?

        IF YES: b Why was maintenance required?
                     c Who did the maintenance?
                     d What was the cost of the work?

8 Current price charged:

                                         LS   per

9 a Over the past year, has the sale price of your water increased?

        IF YES: b Price increased from: LS .   per
                                        to: LS .   per
                     c Date of increase:
                     d Reason for increase:

10 a Is the current sale price of your water adequate?

        IF NO: What price do you think would be adequate?

                                         LS .   per

11 ASK IF AT A STANDPIPE

Are you satisfied with	YES	NO	IF NO, GIVE DETAILS
Size of pipe			
Quality of joints			
Type of tap			
Number of taps			
Drainage			
Height of discharge			
Operator seating			
Facilities			
Water pressure			

Any other suggested improvements to design: _____
_____
_____
_____
_____
_____
_____

12 ASK IF AT A BOREWELL:

Are you satisfied with:	YES	NO	IF NO, GIVE DETAILS
Type of pump			
Drainage			
Operator seating			
Facilities			
Yield			
Quality of water			

Any other suggested improvements to design: _____

_____

_____

_____

_____

_____

_____

SUMMARY

A well-designed form is a vital research tool. Use 'closed' questions, with a limited range of answers, for collecting factual information and 'open' questions, where the answers may be very varied, for finding out about attitudes and experiences. In general, closed questions are appropriate for large structured surveys and open questions for preliminary research. The actual wording of questions should be clear and not open to misinterpretation. The order of questions should be arranged to make the interview flow smoothly and the layout of the form should assist the interviewer in recording information accurately. Coding of answers makes later analysis easier and is essential if a computer is to be used for data analysis.

5 CHOOSING THE SAMPLE

At an early stage of survey design, you need to define exactly which group of people, or units, you are interested in. The full group of interest is called the target population. Part 1 of this chapter is about how to decide on and list the target population to make a sampling frame.

Usually there is not enough time or money to interview everybody in the target population; you will need to pick out a part of it — a smaller group which will be similar to the total population. This selection of representative people or units is called a sample. How far a sample accurately represents its target population depends on two things:

- the size of the sample, and

- how you select it.

Part 2 covers sample size, relating this first to cost and then to the accuracy required. Part 3 summarises basic methods and techniques for choosing the sample. This is sub-divided into random and non-random sampling, and repeat sampling methods.

Part 1 The target population

Before choosing a sample, you need to decide who is part of the target population. This choice will depend on the purpose of the study. Exactly who, or what, is the study intended to find out about? If you are studying water collection or stove usage, for example, the target population will probably consist mostly of women. To look at spending priorities, you must include those making decisions on spending. You may want to research objects, or units, rather than people. Examples might be all the farms in a region, the residential plots in a town, or handpumps in a group of villages.

Listing or mapping the target population

Having defined your target population, the next question is whether or not there are complete lists or maps of the people or units you want to survey. Such a list or map is called a sampling frame. Examples of sampling frames are:

- a list of villages or administrative areas,

- a file of standpipe licences issued,

- a list of plot-holders, or

- a map of a town showing individual dwellings.

The ideal sampling frame would list every unit in the target population separately, once and only once. It would not include units outside the target population. In practice, you will find that some information will be incorrect, missing, or out-of-date. There may be too much information — the list may cover a wider population than you need.

The best administrative lists are often those used for collecting tariffs or taxes. But there can be problems with these lists; if individuals stand to benefit or lose by being on the list, this will probably affect its accuracy. How interested are the officials involved in keeping accurate records? Where an adequate list does exist, can you get access to it? Is it kept in a way which lets you identify and contact people?

You can improve your sampling frame by updating or by compiling lists specially for data collection purposes. For example, if you know your frame completely misses out part of the target population, try working out an additional list for the missing part. Suppose that you are studying water sellers, and the official records ignore informal water sellers. You can still use these records to take a sample of official sellers, but you will need to make an additional sampling frame of informal sellers, through discussions with women carrying water.

Maps

Maps present different problems. For example, what should you take as the boundaries of the study area? Boundaries must be identifiable on the ground (for example, paths or streams). It often helps if they match administrative units. When you are using maps to construct your sample, you will need to do some ground checks and updates. This work is very time-consuming and expensive. It means that, in practice, a small-scale research study will have to be concentrated in several small areas. The most effective way of doing this is by using cluster sampling. We will come back to the use of maps later, under this heading.

Part 2: Deciding on sample size

How large must the sample be? Generally, the bigger the sample the more accurate the results. But also, the higher the cost. You have to strike a balance.

Sample size and cost

Realistically, cost is usually the main factor determining sample size. What staff, funds and transport are available? How much time is there to complete the work? The following example indicates the kind of thinking you should go through:

Suppose that three months are allocated for an urban study. There are two full-time staff, plus funds to cover six interviewers for two weeks. How large a sample is possible? As a general rule, you can expect fieldworkers to complete around three to five long interviews (30 to 45 minutes each) per day in an urban household survey. This figure applies to a five to ten page questionnaire, with interviews for each day located quite close together in the same housing area. With a shorter questionnaire needing interviews of say, 15 to 30 minutes, some five to ten interviews per day may be possible. The number will again vary with the need to travel between interviews, callbacks and the quality of the interviewer.

For any reasonably large sample survey, fieldwork should not take up more than 10 per cent to 15 per cent of the time available. The remainder of the time will be taken up in study design, pre-testing, printing of materials, data analysis and report preparation. You should plan to concentrate fieldwork into a maximum period of two weeks. If one full-time staff member is the supervisor, there are a maximum of seven interviewers for the fieldwork. Working five days per week gives

70 interviewer/days. Assuming three to five interviews per person per day, the possible sample size is between 210 and 350.

This rough estimate will become more exact when both the form and sampling method have been drafted and pre-tested. Resist the temptation of trying to do too much. A small sample, properly managed and carefully analysed, is always better than a poorly supervised, large sample which is never fully analysed for lack of time. Will the sample size you can afford answer your research questions? If it will not, then consider how you might either get more resources, or scale down your research questions to something more realistic.

Sample size and accuracy

Once you have an idea of the size of sample you can afford, you can think about the level of accuracy this size of sample will give you, and if this is adequate for your purposes. For exploratory or in-depth work, your aim is to get a 'feel' for a problem. There is no point in using a large sample, so sample sizes in the range of 30 to 50 are normally enough. Such small, informal studies should include units from all sub-groups of interest in the target population. For example, in a study of latrine owners, you could choose a group containing low, middle and upper income owners. The sample size need only be large enough to include, say, ten to fifteen members of all the sub-groups of interest.

With larger samples, you should use more structured non-random methods such as quota sampling, which are suitable for samples of 50 to 100. If you are planning a larger study than this, you should normally be using a random method to choose the sample. On a study of this scale, it is worth setting aside time and money to develop a good sampling frame.

For random sampling methods the decision on sample size becomes a little more complicated. Even so, the choice of sample size is more a matter of judgement than calculation. The main factor is usually the need to look separately at the results for different sub-groups in the target population. Think about the different data tables you aim to produce, then estimate the numbers in each sub-group for the sample size you are considering. Say, for example, you want to breakdown latrine ownership within each housing area in a sanitation survey. You need to make sure that the sample size in each housing area is large enough to allow reliable comparisons. For example, consider this data from a study in South Sudan:

Housing Area Type	N	Complete Latrine %	Partly-built Latrine %	No Latrine %
Informal	68	6	11	83
4th Class	135	13	26	61
3rd Class	78	78	14	8
1st/2ndClass	37	100	0	0

(N = Size of sample in each case.)

The sample size in most areas is well over fifty, so you can have some confidence in looking at separate results for each area. You need not worry about the smaller sample size in '1st/2nd Class' areas because here all households have a complete latrine; you do not need to sub-divide this group. If you want to look in detail at a sub-group in which there are fewer than 30 cases, your sample size is probably too small. For example, you only picked up four informal households with a complete latrine (6 per cent of 68). Suppose you wanted to break down 'complete latrines in informal areas' by latrine materials, then you would need a larger sample.

Confidence intervals

Apart from the need to consider different sub-groups, you must also look at the overall accuracy of your sample estimates. The aim of taking a large random sample is to obtain numerical estimates which tell you about some characteristics of the target population. For example, you may want to get an estimate of average household income, or average household size. Since the sample is only a part of the target population, the values you obtain from the sample will probably differ slightly from the true values for the overall population. One great advantage of random sampling is that you can easily estimate a range of values within which the true target population value is almost certain to fall. This is called a confidence interval and is worked out using the information you obtain from the sample. The confidence interval makes an allowance for chance variations (differences) between the sample you actually take and other samples that you might have taken.

We will explain the use of confidence intervals in Chapter Six, but it is important to explain here that when you are deciding on a sample size, it is advisable to estimate confidence intervals for some of the most important variables you are studying. Do this at the design stage. It is useless to discover that your confidence intervals are too wide and your final estimates are not very accurate, when the fieldwork is complete.

As an example, suppose a main objective of your survey is to estimate the percentage of households in a certain area who own a latrine. How accurate will your results be with a sample of 100 households?

The formula for calculating a confidence interval is as follows:

$$\textbf{Sample percentage plus or minus 2 x } \sqrt{\frac{\textbf{sample \% x (100 - sample \%)}}{\textbf{sample size}}}$$

To estimate the confidence interval you must first make an 'informed guess' (based on your current knowledge and previous informal observations) of the percentage of households that have a latrine — say, 75 per cent. Putting this estimate into the formula gives you the different confidence intervals for different sample sizes. With a sample size of 100, the confidence interval will be between 66.3 and 83.7 per cent, which has a width of 17.4.

The table below gives the confidence interval widths for various sample sizes and percentage estimates. You will see from this how the width of the confidence interval varies with the sample size. The larger the sample, the more precisely you can estimate the target population value. If your sample does in fact give you a value of 75 per cent for latrine ownership, then you can be confident that the value for the whole target population is between 66 per cent and 84 per cent (rounding to the nearest 1 per cent).

Width of Confidence Interval for a Large Simple Random Sample

		Estimated % value		
	5% or 95%	10% or 90%	25% or 75%	50%
Sample Size 100	8.8	12.0	7.4	20.0
250	5.6	7.6	11.0	12.6
500	3.8	5.4	7.8	9.0
1000	2.8	3.8	5.4	6.4
2500	1.8	2.4	2.6	4.0

Having estimated confidence intervals for a few important variables, you will get a feel for the accuracy of your results from the sample size considered. Decide whether the results are accurate enough for your needs. The table will help you to estimate approximate confidence intervals for a range of sample sizes. Notice that the advantage gained by increasing sample size becomes smaller as the sample size gets larger: for example, you greatly improve accuracy by increasing the sample size from 100 to 250, but once you get above 1000, improvements are small.

In general, use confidence intervals with caution. They only measure chance variation from one sample to another. They do not allow for refusals, non-contacts, poor questions and other factors not related to sample size. In practice, this means that you should allow for a wider margin of error in your results.

Part 3: Methods for choosing the sample

Random sampling

We will now look at some of the basic techniques for choosing a random sample. Note that 'random' does not mean haphazard, casual, or careless. In fact, the opposite is true. Random sampling is selection based on chance; all units in the target population have an equal, known chance of being selected. Chance is used for selection systematically, and kept to strictly. As we will see later, non-random sampling is not careless either. Instead, the method of selection follows a pattern and is partly influenced by the judgement of the researcher or fieldworker.

The main reason for using a random sample is to avoid bias. A biased sample gives a misleading picture of the target population, favouring some parts more than others. Robert Chambers, in his book *Rural Development*, gives several examples of bias. 'Tarmac-road' bias occurs when researchers tend to keep close to major roads or paths. People living in remote areas — often the poorest — are then under-represented. 'Project bias' means visiting areas where projects are already in progress. 'Dry season bias' occurs when fieldwork is done only in the dry season. Easier for the researcher, but unlikely to give a representative picture.

If a sample is truly random it will usually be unbiased. Every unit has the same chance of being included, so long as the sampling frame lists the complete target population and there are few refusals or non-contacts. Taking several random samples (using the same method) will give an accurate average estimate over all the samples. Over a large sample, chance errors should have little impact on final results. There are likely to be very few large errors, and these will tend to be balanced out by the more numerous small errors.

For practical reasons, it may not always be possible to use a random sampling approach, but it is important to realise what you sacrifice if you decide to drop the random method. So much for the theory. How can you go about selecting a random sample?

Simple random sample

A simple random sample is the purest form of random sampling (although it is not often used in practice). We can illustrate the basic idea quite simply; imagine that you take the list of individuals or units — the sampling frame — and give each one a number. You write the numbers on individual slips of paper, put them in a bag and mix the slips up thoroughly, and then draw out the number of slips you want for your sample. A time-saving alternative is a random number table. These are included in most sets of statistical tables and in statistics textbooks. Here is an example:

Random Number Table

```
7951 2257 3713 2251 8787 0475 1806 4328 0394 5752 9546 6241 6391 6881 2013
3476 4938 3030 1040 7821 8732 0890 0539 0386 0229 4020 6212 8989 4264 8738
2354 6217 6397 4452 9636 1291 4708 8747 6045 4629 4887 4269 1324 1153 6073
0242 7111 8223 6214 9296 4380 4885 5385 0352 3626 5649 3898 6182 4164 9660
7152 4503 4104 3607 5164 1690 9877 6536 5113 2852 5873 8459 0452 0417 1987

8674 0361 6652 0446 3064 6299 1841 8833 2724 0735 0429 8584 7512 5118 7745
5448 3932 2042 0559 0730 9695 1405 5741 4885 9212 4531 0068 2163 7377 4841
0195 0036 5426 6163 63-8 6222 6989 4217 8397 7608 5562 2517 6124 6646 4251
8622 2115 2035 3945 5851 9531 8145 5798 8519 0361 9972 7441 1017 3108 6730
9247 3019 3527 7094 6336 6141 4270 8019 2283 1068 7485 7303 1168 6489 8338

7281 7885 5968 0933 7984 0072 0986 6746 7654 3451 4140 3014 0576 9320 9674
9578 3588 6639 0837 2435 1674 6491 7476 9462 3399 7713 8569 7936 2455 5786
0902 3244 1865 0817 2651 3265 9238 3982 9620 4769 2699 8218 0757 2916 4790
6694 7834 6977 2494 6370 2960 6446 3761 7348 2963 9572 2594 9246 5777 3427
3963 8453 2735 2488 7338 7199 0123 1688 4832 5658 2039 0149 2963 7342 6971

9924 5962 8787 2350 7622 6882 3558 0002 5031 2048 5381 7814 6943 4356 9218
7602 8191 8803 9179 9883 6747 6531 4312 1230 1696 3402 0171 7489 4374 5623
8749 6178 1446 6811 0639 2677 1887 1643 2326 9557 0534 9593 5645 0505 9063
7068 2917 7773 7084 4255 8967 9551 1753 3843 4353 0402 0876 8955 0546 3184
9229 3526 3321 8093 2705 5240 6586 6909 2197 2376 0974 2578 4116 4068 2803

6514 5832 3404 1545 7948 0701 3431 0113 8833 8977 6616 4059 6770 5729 4481
7903 5704 0840 4383 2213 5569 7118 7388 1566 5476 5770 1514 0886 8029 2994
3914 2116 0966 6078 6407 2039 1946 6162 2616 0030 7163 8631 8880 2017 1173
1223 2886 8408 8447 8420 8927 6830 6983 6706 7148 6619 7548 0003 9979 1393
0123 3306 3774 2533 1187 9589 6392 9912 7889 1933 9723 3626 8304 0073 6793
```

To use the table:

•Choose one direction to read it — up or down, side to side; it doesn't matter which.

•Choose which digits you will use from each four digit set; perhaps the first two if the sampling frame is less than 100, or the first three if it is between 100 and 1000. To choose a single digit, use two-digit pairs beginning with 0, such as 03, 07.

•Pick any starting point and move down or across the table, writing down each number you come to which corresponds to a member of the sampling frame. Ignore all others, including duplicates.

Say you want a sample of eight, from a list of 154. And say you pick the starting point 2699 (ringed in the table). You decide to choose the first three digits of each set, and to move down the column and then to the right. The first three numbers you come to that are within the sequence 1 to 154 will be 053, 040, 097. Then, moving down the next column to the right, you get 006, 014, 017, 087, 151.

Usually, you do not need to assign a number to every unit in your sampling frame. Instead, work out a consistent system for counting through the units.

The next example shows how a large scale map showing plot boundaries can be used to select households for interview.

Simple Random Sample

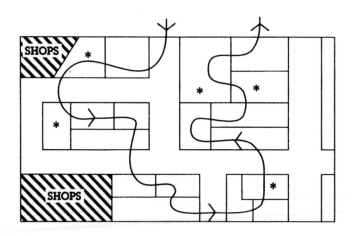

• First, update the map using available records and ground checks.

• Draw a line passing through every plot once (and only once).

• Use the line to count the total number of plots.

• Take random numbers from a random number table. Use the line to count through the units, locating the selected 'numbers' on the map (marked *).

Total: 18 plots, from which you want to select 5. The random numbers from the table, starting at 2699, working down and across as before, taking the last two digits of each number and ignoring any numbers over 18, are 02, 16, 12, 17, 03.

Always make the decisions needed to pick your sample before you start to select numbers. Never change the numbers or redraw the sample because you 'don't like' the numbers selected, or because you think they 'don't look random'. This destroys the basic idea of random selection by pure chance.

We have said that a simple random sample will be free of bias if two conditions are met. First, the sampling frame must be accurate, detailed, and cover the full target population. Second, fieldworkers must succeed in contacting and interviewing all those selected. However, a sample chosen in a truly random way may result in the units selected being widely dispersed, making fieldwork expensive. A further problem is that even an unbiased random sample may actually be unrepresentative, through bad luck; some key sub-groups could be missed out completely. We will look at some straightforward modifications which try to deal with these difficulties.

Systematic samples

One way to make sure the sample is spread evenly through the target population is to use a systematic sample. Here, you select sampling units at regular intervals from the sampling frame, which is often easier to do than selecting units randomly.

For example, using the same map as you used previously, you might decide to select a 20 per cent sample from the 18 plots. Once again, you would draw a line on the map crossing every plot once. But this time you only use random number tables to choose a random starting point. From there, you move across the map, selecting every nth (according to the sample size required) unit for inclusion in the sample. The random number selected from the random number table was 05. To get a 20 per cent systematic sample, you need to select every 4th plot after that (rounded up, 20 per cent of 18 is 4). This time, the selected households would be on plot 5, 9, 13, and 17.

This method is especially useful where a study area contains several distinct sub-groups (such as upper, middle and lower income housing areas), each in different parts of town. For example, to sample housing areas from a large urban area, you can draw the line in a spiral from the centre to the fringe. A systematic sample along this line is likely to include all types of housing area, at different distances from the city centre and at all points of the compass. You can use the same method when sampling plots around a central point of interest (perhaps a communal stand-pipe).

Systematic sample from lists

Some lists are naturally grouped into sections or classes. Town Councillors, for example, may be grouped according to the location of their ward. Stand-pipe licences may be listed by the date of the licence. Systematic sampling then automatically gives you a sample which represents each section or class.

Sometimes information is available to arrange a list in a useful order before you choose the sample. You could arrange a list of villages in order of size, for example, using census data. Then, with a systematic sample, you will be sure of including examples from each category of village size.

To sum up, a systematic sample, like a simple random sample, will normally be free of bias. It has two extra advantages:

- It is easier to select than a simple random sample.

- It is more likely to represent all sub-groups, because you can pre-arrange the sampling frame in sections or classes.

However, it also shares two disadvantages with a simple random sample:

- You still need a detailed, accurate sampling frame for the full target population.

- The units may be widely dispersed, making fieldwork expensive.

Stratified random sample

Next, we will look at a valuable technique to ensure that sub-groups are accurately represented in the sample. A stratified random sample uses existing information to divide the target population into non-overlapping sub-groups (called 'strata'). A random sample is then taken from each sub-group. Members of each sub-group should be similar to each other in some way — perhaps they live in the same village, or have the same kind of job, or have roughly the same income. By taking a simple random sample (or systematic sample) within each sub-group, not only is each sub-group properly represented, it is also easier to compare final survey results for different sub-groups.

You cannot use stratified sampling if you lack sufficient information to decide which sub-group to put the units into. And the method is only useful when you can divide the population into sub-groups which are related to the interests of the study. The following characteristics are examples of characteristics which are often useful for dividing a target population into sub-groups:

•Settlement size, to stratify a target population of villages, towns and cities. Use census data to list settlements into each size sub-group, then draw a separate sample from each sub-group.

•Ecological zone, for example, to stratify a target population of farms. Divide a map showing farm boundaries into ecological zones, then sample farms from each zone separately.

•Housing area, to stratify a target population of urban households. Divide a map showing plot divisions into housing areas, then sample plots from each housing area separately.

•Distance, to stratify a population by distance from a central point. For example, to study usage of a new borewell, draw distance zones on a map; less than 500 metres from the borewell, 500 to 1,000 metres away, or over 1,000 metres away. Then sample separately from each distance zone.

•Presence of key facilities. For example, to study the effectiveness of a health programme, mark all health centres on a map of the study area. Allocate each village to a sub-group by presence or absence of a health centre, dispensary or referral centre, then sample separately from each health facility's sub-group.

61

How should you divide up the total sample between sub-groups? The simplest method is according to the share of the total target population in each sub-group; a sub-group containing one quarter of the target population is allocated one quarter of the total sample size. Suppose you had a target population of 200 people, and your planned sample size is 40. Here, the low income group consists of 130 people, which is 65 per cent of the total. Within your sample of 40, you should select 26 from this group (0.65 x 40).

Sub-Group	No. in each sub-group	% of target population in each sub-group	Sample size for each sub-group
Low Income	130	65	26
Middle Income	56	28	11
Upper Income	14	7	3
	200	100	40

You will often want to compare results for each sub-group. In order to do so, you may need to over-sample in those sub-groups with a small total population. If you do this, you will then need to weight the results from individual sub-groups according to their size relative to the whole population, when they are re-combined to give an overall average.

For example, if you wanted to compare the percentage of households who own a latrine in each of the different income groups, you would first have to ensure that the samples for each group were large enough to be representative; here you would need to take more examples from the upper income group.

If the results you obtained for percentage of households with latrine were 14 per cent, 32 per cent and 78 per cent for the three income groups, to get an estimate of the percentage of households with a latrine in the total population you would have to weight the estimates for the individual groups by their relative size in the population:

Low income: 14% x .65 = 9.1
Middle income: 32% x .28 = 9.0
Upper income: 78% x .07 = 5.5

% of total population with latrine = 23.6%

To sum up, stratified sampling is a cost effective method of increasing the accuracy of your survey:

•It lets you use your existing knowledge about the target population to make sure key sub-groups are accurately represented in the sample.

•You can fix the sample size in advance for each sub-group to make sure of getting a representative sample.

The disadvantages of stratified sampling are:

•You need enough information about the complete target population to be able to divide it into sub-groups.

•You need to use weights when you combine results for different sub-groups.

Cluster sampling

Cluster sampling is similar to simple random sampling, but instead of selecting from individual sampling units in a total target population, you select from clusters of units. This method will usually result in major savings in travel costs and time, and you can therefore interview a larger sample. It means you only need a detailed sampling frame, accurately listing or mapping individual population units, for the selected clusters.

For example, if you were sampling households in an area where they were grouped together in isolated settlements, it would be more economical in terms of travel cost to interview all the households in randomly selected settlements rather than the same number of households randomly selected from all the different settlements.

In a rural study you could select a sample of villages (the clusters) at random, from the census list and hold all the interviews in these selected villages. In an urban study you may decide to select individual housing areas as the clusters. Stratify the list of clusters before you select areas for interview. For example, in a rural study, group villages by size and select one or more villages from each size grouping.

Always use cluster sampling with caution. Because you are concentrating your sample in small areas within the target population, it is easy to miss out some important sub-groups completely. The rules are:

• Before you choose the sample, arrange the list of clusters into similar sub-groups of about the same size.

• Use many small clusters rather than a few large ones.

• Number each cluster.

• Using random numbers, select a sample of complete clusters. The exact total sample size depends on the clusters selected, but if clusters are roughly equal in size, this is not a problem.

• Fieldworkers interview every household/individual in the selected clusters.

Using maps

At the beginning of this chapter, we said that maps can present problems, especially in the time and expense needed for ground checks and updating. Using a cluster sample saves a lot of this work.

You will still need an overall 'feel' for demographic changes. In rural areas, check if villages have moved, disappeared or been renamed. In urban areas, check on the ground to see if new housing areas have developed or old ones filled in. Where are the new boundaries? For both urban housing areas and villages, you will need a rough population estimate as well as outline location information for the full study area. However, you will only need to carry out detailed mapping and updating work in the selected clusters, to ensure that every plot is located by fieldworkers.

A further problem is that, although large-scale maps, up to about 1:5000 scale, show individual plots and buildings, your target population probably consists of people and households. You need to decide who, within a building or compound, is selected for interview. One solution is on-the-spot random selection of an eligible household member by the fieldworkers using the Kish Selection Grid:

The Kish Selection Grid

Selection Number	Total number in household eligible for interview					
	1	2	3	4	5	6 or more
1 or 2	1	1	2	2	3	3
3	1	2	3	3	3	5
4 or 5	1	2	3	4	5	6
6	1	1	1	1	2	2
7 or 8	1	1	1	1	1	1
9	1	2	3	4	5	5
10 or 11	1	2	2	3	4	4
12	1	1	1	2	2	2

The Kish Selection Grid can be used when a household includes more than one eligible person. With the grid, a fieldworker can make a random, on-the-spot selection. It works like this:

•Each form has a selection number printed on it, from 1 to 12. There are a roughly equal number of forms with each selection number.

•The fieldworker lists all those eligible for interview in a standard order; usually males, then females, from the oldest down. The fieldworker gives each person a number, working down the list.

•The fieldworker then reads along the line for the given form selection number until reaching the column for the correct total number of eligible people. She or he then reads off the person number for interview.

An alternative approach is to split the fieldwork into two stages. First, visit all the sampled areas (or buildings) to prepare a list of all eligible people for interview. Use this list to randomly select your final sample, then return to complete the full interviews.

Two-stage sample

For large clusters, such as complete towns or villages, you may want to take a further sample within each cluster. This is called two-stage sampling. First, the clusters are selected using random sampling. If the size of the clusters is the same, then this can be done by simply allocating a number to each cluster and using a random number table. If the clusters are of different sizes, then the usual procedure is to choose clusters in such a way that the probability of their being selected is in proportion to their size. If one cluster has twice as large a population as another, it is given twice the chance of being selected.

For example, if there are five districts — the clusters — within a town, each containing different percentages of the total population, you would assign numbers from 1 to 100 according to this percentage as follows:

Cluster	% of population in cluster	numbers assigned to cluster for random sampling
1	8	1 - 8
2	12	9 - 20
3	16	21 - 36
4	30	37 - 66
5	34	67 - 100

Using a random number table might give you the numbers 18, 39 and 71, so you would choose the clusters 2, 4 and 5.

In either case, once the clusters have been selected, the same number of people are usually sampled from each cluster. Any sampling method can be used at this second stage.

Other sampling methods increase the complexity of the design and analysis. It is therefore advisable to seek reliable statistical advice, perhaps from the national statistical office. Normally, you should not need to use complicated methods for small-scale project studies. (Look at the Bibliography for further reading on sampling methods.)

To summarise, cluster sampling and two-stage methods have the advantages that you need a less detailed sampling frame than for simpler sampling methods, and you can reduce travel costs. The main disadvantages are that sample design and data analysis become more complicated, and that, by chance, important sub-groups can be missed out of the sample.

The random walk

Before we move to non-random methods of sampling, we will look at the 'Random Walk', used for sampling plots or households. (In fact, this is not entirely random, as it relies on the thoroughness and judgement of the fieldworker.)

Fieldworkers are given detailed, precise instructions to follow a set route, interviewing households at regular intervals. For example:

- From the starting point, go north as directly as possible.

- Take the first road on your right.

- Interview at the second plot on your left.

- Continue along the road in the same direction.

- Pass ten plots on your right and interview at the next, and so on.

Tell fieldworkers to follow the instructions exactly. You can include instructions on selecting a household within the plot or an individual within the household. If you do, insist that they must call back if the appropriate respondent is not there, otherwise there will be serious bias in the sample.

This method only works well in neatly laid out, dispersed settlements. It is often difficult to work out clear random walk instructions for the haphazard layouts of many rural villages or urban housing areas. There is also a danger of a 'tarmac-road bias' of a sort: plots approached by small paths and far from roads may be ignored.

Non-random methods of sampling

Random sampling has great advantages in theory. In practice, its value is limited by the quality of your sampling frame and the need to keep fieldwork costs low. These are the usual reasons for using non-random sampling instead.

Non-random sampling is any form of selection based completely or partly on the judgement of the fieldworker or researcher. Non-random methods by-pass the work involved in developing a sampling frame and speed up the process of locating people to interview in the field. However, the methods are not objective and can produce significant bias unless used with care. Having said this, random sampling has little advantage for very small samples. To select a few case-study households you may prefer to rely on your own judgment, rather than leave the choice to a random method which will involve constructing a full sampling frame.

The simplest form of non-random sample is the purposive (or judgmental) sample. To draw up a purposive sample you make an informed judgment about what is 'typical' in the target population or sub-group of interest. For example, in a small rural case study, you could use this method to choose one or two villages with 'typical' health problems. This method is only valuable for sampling a very small number of units. It means that your experience and knowledge (guided by relevant experts) becomes crucial. The danger is that you have no way of knowing how typical your sample really is.

Quota sample

A more advanced approach to non-random sampling is the quota sample. This uses information about the target population to describe, in a general way, the types of people (or units) to be included in the sample. Each interviewer is given a quota of certain types of people with whom to complete interviews, but the final choice of who to interview in the field is left to her or his own judgement. This removes the need for a sampling frame.

When choosing a person (or unit) the fieldworker is told to look for characteristics called quota controls. Physical or observable features make the best quota controls. Age and sex fall into this category, as do house type and location (region, village or housing area). For example, using age and sex, you might give a fieldworker the following quota to fill:

Number of Interviews

	Male	Female	% of Population
10 - 19 years	10	10	16
20 - 29 years	12	12	20
30 - 39 years	15	15	24
40 + years	25	25	40

To design a quota sample you must know, at least approximately, how the target population is divided up according to the quota controls. In this example you would use age and sex data from the census or from an earlier survey to decide on the numbers you need to include in each category.

The sample will only accurately represent the target population in terms of the quota controls you have used. For example, using physical quota controls, such as age and sex, cannot guarantee a balanced sample in social and economic terms. In other words, there is no reason to suppose the sample will accurately represent the target population in factors such as income level, house type, or ethnic group.

Two examples of how of quota sampling could be used in small, exploratory studies are:

- In a study of informal water sellers: specify a small quota of informal sellers in each housing area, based on the number of on-plot water-supplies (available from water authority records). Fieldworkers locate their quota through conversations with those carrying water.

- In a detailed study of latrine-owners: use previous survey data to specify quotas by housing area and latrine construction materials. Assuming latrines are easily visible from the road, fieldworkers can then cycle around each housing area to locate the specified quota.

Quota sampling has two major advantages. First, you do not need a detailed sampling frame. Second, anybody who fits the quota controls can be interviewed. So there is no need for callbacks to contact a respondent not present. We have already mentioned the disadvantage that you need detailed information on the target population to set up quota controls. You will also find such controls difficult to use when looking at topics like income or employment. You will need to carry out preliminary interviews, checking with possible respondents to see whether they fall into a quota group.

There may be other problems. Interviewers can fail to fill their quota, especially if the controls are complicated. Also, bias may go undetected. Interviewers can bend the rules, or the information used to set up quota controls may be out-of-date. Finally, many researchers see quota sampling as less 'respectable' than random methods. Quota sampling is not often used in development work, but it can sometimes be useful, especially in small studies where physical or observable features are of key interest (as in many housing studies).

Genealogy-based sample

The genealogy-based sample selects entire families, including all close relatives, rather than individual households. In rural areas this can give you a reasonable cross-section of the community by age and sex, without involving the use of a sampling frame. Use an initial contact to get in touch with all relatives in turn, wherever they are living. If it is not practical to visit all related families, it will usually be possible to collect at least some of the information you need about them from your initial contacts.

This method has given reasonable results in self-contained, traditional villages where social and economic differences between families are small. It has obvious drawbacks in studies which investigate factors where there are stronger similarities between family members than between individuals from different families.

Chain sampling

Chain — also called snowball — sampling can be useful for rare or minority units. Make your first contact with a member of the target population through friends, colleagues, or perhaps through data from a previous survey. Interview the first contact, then ask if they know any other members of the target population. The low-income latrine owner, for example, could be asked whether any of his friends have also built a latrine. Follow up every contact mentioned; interview them and ask them for further contacts. You hope that each new contact will know extra members of the target population as well as the person that put them on the list.

Examples of rare or minority target populations include:

• informal water sellers,

• owners of particular types of small business,

• women who brew or distil, or

• types of local craftsmen, such as thatchers or builders.

Matched samples

Matched samples are useful if you need to compare two sub-groups which are alike in some way. For example, you can choose a matched pair of villages, with similar populations and services (schools, health centres, borewells, etc). If you study a new project in just one of a matched pair, the other unit is a control against which you can compare changes in the project area. In order to be sure that the differences you detect are due to the new project and not due to something else, care must be taken to match for every possible influencing factor.

Repeat sampling methods

This section looks at approaches to the repeated collection of data. You often need a picture of changes over time. For an agricultural study you will need to collect information at different phases of the season or times of the year. Urban plot construction will vary between wet and dry seasons. You may want to observe the pattern of stand-pipe usage during the early morning, in the heat of the day, in late afternoon and perhaps even at night.

Panel survey

A panel is a set of people (or units) which you visit several times over a long time period. For instance, you could set up a panel of farmers and visit them through a full season, collecting a wide range of detailed information at regular intervals. The panel survey cuts down the work involved in sample selection; you only need to select one sample (i.e. the panel) for the whole set of repeat visits. But this has its dangers. A major problem is that members of the panel lose interest in the study. If some drop out, this can produce bias.

Another danger is that members can actually change the way they act because they are in the study. Finally, over time, changes in the target population will not always be reflected in the panel.

Repeat survey

The repeat survey avoids most of these problems. It means that the entire process, including sample selection, is repeated. But it has some problems; it is more time-consuming and expensive than a panel survey. Also, you need a larger sample size if you are to make accurate comparisons over time. While the panel survey automatically compares like with like, in a repeat survey changes over time may become confused with random changes, in the sample used.

The rotating survey

The rotating survey is a mixture of the two previous approaches. A fraction of the panel (say, one fourth) is changed on each visit. Each panel member is interviewed a fixed number of times, then leaves the panel. There is less danger of the panel members losing interest. Also, because the panel is always taking in new people, it can reflect changes in the target population better than a simple panel survey. Even so, changes in the panel happen slowly, so real changes over time stand out clearly from random changes in panel membership.

SUMMARY

Before beginning a survey, you need to decide on the exact target population in which you are interested. From this, you need to select a sample of people or units to survey. The aim is to select a sample that represents the target population as accurately as possible.

The availability of survey staff and the required project timescale are key factors affecting your choice of sampling method and the size of sample. Careful sample design, and good survey management, will improve the reliability of the survey results whatever size of sample you choose.

There are many different ways of choosing a sample. Random sampling is selection based on chance, where all units of the target population have an equal, known chance of inclusion in the sample. Using a random method -- whether a simple, stratified or clustered design is chosen -- is the most reliable way to reduce selection bias to a minimum level.

With a random sample design you will be able to estimate whether or not the size of sample you can afford to work with will be accurate enough for your purposes. This involves the use of confidence intervals -- the range of values for a particular variable (factor or attribute) within which the true value for the total population is almost certain to fall. Well-designed, larger samples have smaller confidence intervals, so the survey results are more reliable.

The alternative is to choose a non-random approach, such as purposive, quota or chain sampling. Non-random methods tend to be cheaper and quicker than random sampling. They can be useful for selecting a small sample, where a rapid appraisal is necessary. The drawback is that non-random methods generally involve some deliberate judgement on the part of the fieldworker, so the risk of bias is increased.

6 TECHNIQUES FOR DATA ANALYSIS

This chapter outlines some simple tools for analysing survey information. Tables, percentages and averages give a clear picture of the sample data, particularly for non-specialists, and many of the users of your research will only be interested in this level of analysis.

We will also look at measures of spread, including percentiles and standard deviations, which give a picture of how the variable you are interested in is distributed throughout the sample population. You will find more about these in most mathematical or statistical textbooks. Finally, we outline some of the most frequently used graphs and charts which both illustrate and help to analyse numerical data.

In most small-scale surveys, aiming at rapid, straightforward results, you will be able to go a long way using these basic methods. If you are doing a good deal of social survey work, it is worth taking a practical course in statistics. If possible, take advice from a specialist statistician when planning your survey and before starting analysis of your data.

Variables and tables

A variable is a single characteristic of the target population. Variables used in examples in this book include household size and household income. Each variable has a single value for each unit in the target population. For example, the value of the variable 'household size' for a particular unit is simply the number of people in the household.

We can break down a sample, or part of a sample, using just one variable. The table produced is called a one-way table. Here is an example where 71 households are shown according to the number of rooms they rented:

Number of Rooms Rented per Household

Number of Rooms	Number of Households
1	43
2	19
3 or more	9
TOTAL	**71**

By sorting households like this, we have distributed our sample according to the characteristic — the variable — chosen. For any sample, the full set of sample values for a particular variable is called a distribution. There is another way of putting this. We can say that the 'number of households' column gives the frequency of the variable ('number of rooms') i.e. how often it occurs within the sample that households rent one room, two rooms, etc. So a one-way table is sometimes called a frequency distribution table.

A two-way table involves categorising the data in terms of two variables. This is also called cross-tabulation. It is the basic tool used to look at the relationship between two variables. For example:

Rent Paid by Number of Rooms Rented

Number of Rooms Rented	Rent Paid Monthly ($)				
	0-9	10-14	15-19	20-24	30+
1	14	22	6	1	0
2	2	1	6	8	2
3+	0	1	0	5	3

Percentages

The percentage is a simple and widely understood statistic. It gives a good 'feel' for how a variable within a sample is distributed over categories. Suppose that, in a sample of 58 households, there were 16 households with a monthly income between $0-$49. We can state this proportion as the fraction $\frac{16}{58}$. To change this to a percentage, simply multiply by one hundred; i.e. proportion x 100 = percentage. In this case, $\frac{16}{58}$ x 100 = 27.59.

Rounding up, the percentage of the sample with a monthly income between $0-$49 is 28 per cent.

In a one-way table we can make the same calculation for each subgroup. The percentage of units in a sub-group is the number of units that would fall in that sub-group if the sample size was exactly 100. We can express the results in the form of a table. For example:

Number of Rooms Rented per Household

Number of Rooms	Number of Households (frequency)	% Households
1	43	60
2	19	27
3 or more	9	13
TOTAL	**71**	**100**

Percentages are also a useful tool when examining two-way tables:

	% in each Rent Category					
Number of Rooms Rented	$0 - 9	$10 - 14	$15 - 19	$20 - 29	$30+	N
1	33	51	14	2	0	43
2	11	5	31	42	11	19
3 or more	0	11	0	56	33	9

In a two-way table, one variable ('number of rooms rented') is expressed in terms of another variable ('rent paid'); in this example, of the 60 per cent of households in the sample who rent one room, 33 per cent pay under $9, 51 per cent pay between $10 and $14, etc. (Note that the percentages total 100 for each of these 'number of rooms' categories.)

The 'N' or 'number' column gives the sample size for each 'number of rooms' category. Always include the relevant sample sizes on a table of percentages. This gives readers an idea of how accurate the figures are likely to be. More important, a percentage is meaningless unless we know the base; what is it a percentage of? An exact percentage of an unknown number is still an unknown number! Don't calculate percentages for very small total sample sizes (say, less than thirty). They give a false impression of accuracy.

Averages

The average is a measure of where the centre, or middle, of a distribution lies. In statistics there are two commonly used forms of average: the mean and the median. The mean is how we usually understand the word average in simple arithmetic: add up a set of items and then divide that total by the number of items in the set. The median is the middle value when the data are arranged in order of size.

To illustrate both, look at the table below. It shows the variable 'total monthly household income' from a sample of 58 households. The values are arranged in order of size:

0	40	54	80	120	180
0	40	55	82	125	208
15	41	55	82	125	208
19	45	60	95	145	230
20	48	60	105	150	230
20	49	60	110	150	250
30	50	63	114	160	300
36	53	64	115	165	563
40	54	68	118	170	
40	54	71	120	175	

The mean is the sum of the values of the variable divided by the sample size. In this case, adding the values together and dividing by 58 gives a mean of $103.1

Now, the median. As there are an even number of households in the sample (58), there is no single middle value. So we estimate the median as the mid-point between the 29th value ($68) and 30th value ($71). The estimated median is $69.50.

In this case, the median and the mean have quite different values. Which is the best average? The mean is a kind of imaginary centre for the distribution. If every household in the sample dropped their monthly income into a box and the money was redistributed equally, each would then have the mean income. In our example, this is not a very useful definition of the centre of the distribution as no household actually receives this amount and unless we return to the table of values, we do not know how many households receive less than the monthly mean income. Not only that, the mean is not very 'robust'; that is, it is easily influenced by extreme (possibly erroneous) values. By removing just one household from the sample, the household with an income of $563, the mean will become 93, which is a large reduction. The example shows a typical situation where the mean income is pulled up by a few richer families to a level well above the median.

In contrast, the median tells us something very concrete: half the sample have an income of less than $70 (to the nearest dollar) and half the sample have an income of more than $70. This seems a useful definition of the centre of distribution. The median has another advantage. It is a robust measure i.e. it is not so easily influenced by extreme values, so small changes in the sample will not change the median very much.

Though the median is the more useful average measure in this example, it has disadvantages. It can be time consuming to arrange a large number of values in order of size. With a calculator, it is usually quicker to work out the mean.

Grouped data

You can only calculate the exact mean when your data gives you exact numerical values for a variable. But often, fieldworkers do not write exact values on the form. Suppose the data from the last sample was grouped as below:

Total Household Income, Informal Areas

Monthly Income($) between	No. of Households (frequency)
0 - 49	16
50 - 99	18
100 - 149	10
150 - 199	7
200 - 299	5
300 - 399	1
400 - 599	1

As there are 58 households, we know the median is between the 29th and 30th largest values. So, for our grouped data, the median falls within the second income group, $50-99. But this is too wide to be of much practical value by itself.

To get a single, more precise estimate, we must assume that the 18 values are evenly spread within this class. First, divide the class width (49) by the class frequency (18). This gives 2.7, which represents the estimated interval between values, if all the values were evenly spread. The 29th value in the whole series of 58 is the 13th value in this particular class, and will have a value of 50 + (13 x 2.7) = 85.39. The 30th reading will be 50 + (14 x 2.7) = 87.8. The median is the midpoint between these two values, which is 86.6. As the true median is $69.50, we can see this is not an exact method, though it is an improvement on the median income group (50 to 99). Its accuracy depends on whether

77

our assumption that the values within this class are evenly spread, is correct.

Next, the mean. In order to find a single representative value, we have to make an assumption that the exact income of each household lies at the mid-point of the income group concerned:

Income group	Income Group Mid-point	Number of Households
0 - 49	24.5	16
50 - 99	74.5	18
100 - 149	124.5	10
150 - 199	174.5	7
200 - 299	249.5	5
300 - 399	349.5	1
400 - 599	499.5	1

The estimated mean is therefore:

$$\frac{(16 \times 24.5) + (18 \times 74.5) + (10 \times 124.5) + (7 \times 174.5) + (5 \times 249.5) + 349.5 + 499.5}{58}$$

$$= \frac{6296}{58}$$

$$= 108.55$$

So long as the values are well-distributed within the class boundaries, this method works fairly well. In this case, we know that the true value for the mean (using exact values) is $103.1

Measures of spread

The average of a set of data gives a measure of where the centre of a distribution lies. But it gives no idea of how spread out (dispersed) or compact the distribution is. Look at these two distributions:

Group A: 8, 9, 10, 11, 12
Group B: 0, 5, 10, 15, 20

Both distributions have the same mean and median (10), but there is a big difference in the amount of spread around the average value.

The simplest measure of spread is the range. To find the range of a set of data, subtract the lowest value in the data from the highest value. For

78

example, for the income data in the last section, the range is: 563 - 0 = $563. However, this alone is rarely a useful summary measure of spread. Because it depends on just two values, it can often be misleading.

A more useful measure is the interquartile range. Just as the median (the middle value) divides the full range of values into two halves, you can further divide it into quarters. The three values which do this are called quartiles. The middle quartile is the same as the median; the median of the upper half of the data is called the upper quartile and the median of the lower half of the data is the lower quartile. The interquartile range is found by subtracting the lower quartile from the upper quartile. In the example of income data, the lower and upper quartiles are $48 (the 15th value) and $145 (the 44th value). This gives an interquartile range of $97.

Percentiles

You may sometimes want to divide a sample into a number of equal sized groups. The most commonly used measure is the percentile, when a sample is divided into 100 equal sized groups. Here is an example, using the income data above:

To find the 60th percentile:

- Divide the sample size by 100. Leave the answer as a decimal. (Here, the sample size is 58, so dividing by 100 gives 0.58.)

- Multiply the answer by the percentile number you want. (Multiplying by 60 gives 34.8.)

- This tells you between which two values the percentile lies. (The 60th percentile is $\frac{8}{10}$ of the way between the 34th and 35th largest values.)

- Subtract the smaller from the larger of the two values. (The smaller (34th) value is $95. The larger (35th) value is $105. Subtracting 95 from 105 gives 10.)

- Multiply the difference by the required fraction. (Multiplying 10 by the fraction $\frac{8}{10}$ gives 8.)

• Add the result to the smaller value. This gives you the 60th percentile. (Adding 8 to 95 tells us that the 60th percentile is 103.) For grouped data, you can use a similar method for that used to estimate the median.

Percentiles are a useful, practical tool, especially with income data. You might want to define a project target group as the 25 per cent of households in the study area with the lowest income. You know that 25 per cent of the sample earn less than the 25th percentile level. Using the data in the example, the 25th percentile (the lower quartile) is $48. So you may estimate that 25 per cent of households have a total monthly income of $48 or less.

Percentiles are not directly related to measures of spread, but we mention them here for the sake of completeness.

The standard deviation

The standard deviation, like the mean, takes into account all the observed values in the sample; whereas the median and the various ranges rely on particular values. The standard deviation gives an indication of the average amount that values in a particular sample deviate from the mean value. A deviation is the size of the difference between two numbers. For example, the deviation of 8 from 9 is 1. A deviation from the mean is the size of the difference between a value in a distribution and the mean of that distribution.

To return to the two distributions we looked at earlier:

Group A: 8, 9, 10, 11, 12
Group B: 0, 5, 10, 15, 20

Both these distributions have a mean of 10. If we subtract the mean from the value in each case, we obtain the following table:

Group A:		Group B:	
Value	Deviation from the mean	Value	Deviation from the mean
8	-2	0	-10
9	-1	5	-5
10	0	10	0
11	1	15	5
12	2	20	10

80

Notice that some deviations have a minus value. However, we are interested in the size of the deviations, not their direction. To calculate the standard deviation, we square each deviation (that is, multiply it by itself) and then take the mean of the summed squared deviations, which is called the variance. The square root of the variance gives the standard deviation.

The two deviations now look like this:

Value	Deviations from the mean	Squared deviation
Group A:		
8	-2	-2 x -2 = 4
9	-1	-1 x -1 = 1
10	0	0 x 0 = 0
11	1	1 x 1 = 1
12	2	2 x 2 = 4
Group B:		
0	-10	-10 x -10 = 100
5	-5	-5 x -5 = 25
10	0	0 x 0 = 0
15	5	5 x 5 = 25
20	10	10 x 10 = 100

For Group A above the mean of the squared deviations — the variance — is $\frac{10}{5} = 2$; for Group B the mean is $\frac{250}{5} = 50$. The square root of the variance gives us the standard deviation. For Group A above, the standard deviation is the square root of 2 = 1.41. For group B, the standard deviation is the square root of 50 = 7.07.

The standard deviation is an important, commonly used summary measure. Using it together with the mean gives a much clearer description of the data. The shared mean of these two groups told us that they have the same centre. The standard deviations now show that the second distribution is spread far more widely around this centre.

Without a computer, it is very time-consuming to work out standard deviations for large samples. One short cut is to use grouped data. Even when you have exact values, arrange the data in groups. Then assume that all the values in each group are at the mid-point of the group. Though this produces small inaccuracies, it is enormously time-saving.

An even simpler short-cut is to use a calculator with statistical functions. You key in the data (usually as grouped data) and the calculator computes both mean and standard deviation.

Standard deviation in practice

When do we use standard deviations in practice? In Chapter Five, we touched on the use of confidence intervals to estimate how reliably a sample represented the target population. It is time to look at this again, in more detail.

Standard deviations give an idea of how reliable the sample averages and percentages are, as statements about the target population. If there is a lot of spread in the sample (the standard deviation is large) you cannot make a very accurate statement about the whole target population from summary measures of the sample. The sample could easily be very different.

First, the sample average. Using the standard deviation and the sample size, we can estimate a range within which the whole target population average is almost certain to fall. This is the confidence interval. The formula for a confidence interval for a sample average is:

$$\textbf{sample average plus or minus 2}\left(\frac{\textbf{standard deviation}}{\sqrt{\textbf{sample size}}}\right)$$

Taking the example of a sample of 58 households, where the mean income is $103.1 and the standard deviation $90.53, the confidence interval for the mean household income level in the target population is:

103.1 plus or minus 2x $\dfrac{90.53}{\sqrt{58}}$

= $103.1 plus or minus $23.8

= $79 to $127 approximately.

We can be reasonably certain that the true mean household income level falls within this range.

Now the sample percentage. The formula for a confidence interval for a sample percentage is:

Sample percentage plus or minus 2x $\sqrt{\dfrac{\textbf{sample \% x (100 - sample \%)}}{\textbf{sample size}}}$

For example, say 50 per cent of households in a sample of 58 have a monthly household income of less than $69.5. The confidence interval for this percentage is:

50 plus or minus 2x $\sqrt{\dfrac{\textbf{50 x 50}}{\textbf{58}}}$

= 50% plus or minus 13.2%

= 37% to 63%, approximately.

Incomes in these examples vary widely. The standard deviation is large and the sample size low. Both the confidence intervals are quite wide. You would not want to rely on such inexact sample results, where you need precise information about a target population, for example, to design a loans scheme.

Some more graphs and charts

Graphs are a helpful way of exploring data. We will look at three common examples: the bar chart, histogram and scatter diagram. (A further common diagram — the pie chart— is shown in Chapter Eight)

Bar chart

A bar chart is a graph where the length of each bar varies with the data it represents. Bars can be drawn horizontally or vertically, whichever is convenient. Label both the bars and their lengths, showing the units of measurement. One axis will represent the frequency or percentage and the other will represent the particular categories.

Monthly Household Income figures, for example, could be shown in this way. A bar would chart plainly illustrate their overall pattern. Notice that the widths, and the spaces between bars, are the same.

Bar Chart of Monthly Household Income

Monthly income ($)

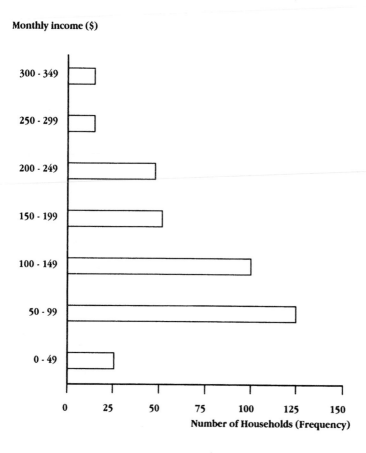

Histogram

Histograms are used to illustrate data which is grouped. Histograms are similar to bar charts, except that the bars will be touching and their areas are very important.

Usually, the sub-groups of data will have the same range, therefore the width of the bars will be the same, and their heights will represent the frequencies (numbers in each sub-group). As the area of a bar is the width times the height, if two sub-groups have the same frequency, the bars representing them will have the same height and so the same area.

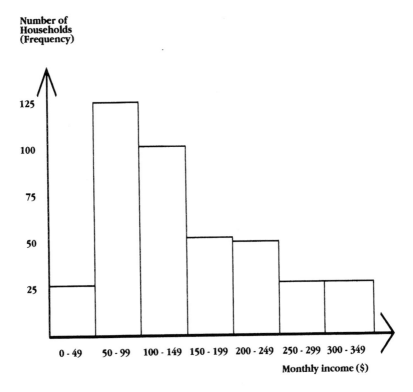

Histogram of Monthly Household Income

Number of
Households
(Frequency)

125

100

75

50

25

0 - 49   50 - 99   100 - 149   150 - 199   200 - 249   250 - 299   300 - 349

Monthly income ($)

In the example above, the subgroups of monthly income have the same range, so the bars have the same width:

However, if the range of two sub-groups differ but their frequencies are the same, making the bars of equal height will not produce the same area. It is therefore necessary to adjust the heights. As an example, suppose the sub-groups 100 to 149 and 150 to 249 both have a frequency of 100. In order to ensure the areas of the bars representing them are the same, the height of the block for the 150-249 sub-group will need to be 5, and the height of the 100 to 149 group 10 i.e. 100 x 5 = 50 x 10. This is shown in the diagram overleaf. Note that where the sub-groups are unequal, there is no vertical axis. Instead, the frequency of each sub-group is written above its bar:

85

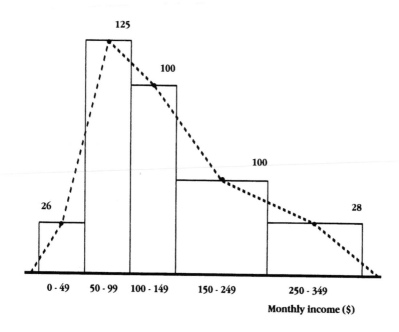

This illustration also uses a line graph to show the general shape of a histogram. Draw the graph by first marking the mid-point of the top of each bar. Mark the mid-points of imaginary extra bars on the horizontal axis at each end. Join the marked points with a straight line. Line graphs are useful if you want to compare two histograms.

Scatter diagram

If you are studying the relationship between two numerical variables which have exact values, a scatter diagram is often more helpful than a two-way table. Plot each pair of sample values on to a graph. Make sure you label each axis, and mark the scale of values for each variable. The example below plots 'income' against 'years in full time education':

Where the points seem to fall along a line (straight or curved), this suggests a relationship between the two variables, (although this relationship may not be causal). In the example above, no relationship is suggested.

Scatter Diagram

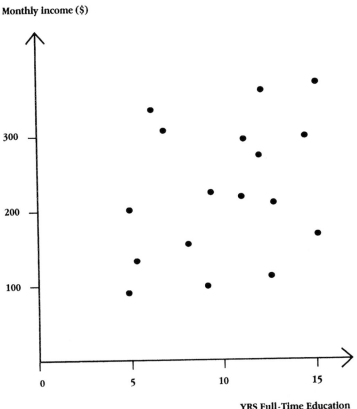

Going further

Statistical methods have been developed to measure the strength of relationship between such exact numerical variables. More about these methods — correlation and regression analysis — can be found in books listed in the Bibliography.

SUMMARY

The information collected from a survey can be analysed in different ways. Table are a useful way of summarising survey findings. A one-way table, or frequency distribution, shows how one particular variable is distributed over the sample; a two-way table (cross-tabulation) uses a second variable to further sub-divide the sample. In order to compare sub-groups, they can be expressed as percentages of the total sample or category.

An average is a measure of the middle of a distribution. Two useful averages are the mean (the sum of values divided by the sample size) and the median (the middle value of series).

Another important aspect of a distribution is the degree of spread — how much the values for a variable spread out around the centre. The range is the difference between the highest and lowest value. The interquartile range is the difference between the upper quartile value (half way between the top of the range and the median) and the lower quartile value (half way between the median and the bottom of the range). The standard deviation is a very useful statistical tool; it is an indication of the average amount of spread in a sample.

Charts or graphs are other ways of summarising survey results. Examples are bar-charts, histograms and scatter diagrams.

7 DATA ANALYSIS

This chapter concentrates on data analysis for structured surveys. For informal research methods, data tables and summary measures such as averages and measures of spread are less useful because much of the information is not in numerical form and sample sizes are often very small.

The information collected during survey fieldwork is called raw data. Generally, it has little practical value as it stands, and you will expect to go through these four stages of processing and analysis:

- Checking through the forms and correcting errors.

- Coding.

- Preparing data tables.

- Making sense of the data. This includes preparing summary measures, and using them to test ideas about the target population.

Before we look at these stages, there are some general points to bear in mind. First, and most important, this guide to data analysis does not involve complicated statistical methods. For small-scale surveys, the methods outlined in Chapter Six will probably be all you need. These are familiar tools like averages, percentages, tables and — less often — measures of spread such as standard deviation.

Second, even when data analysis is straightforward, it is still time-consuming. The temptation is usually to plan to do too much. So be cautious and don't underestimate the work involved. In particular, you should plan data analysis carefully before fieldwork begins. For example, make sure that the list of tables you aim to produce (the tabulation plan) is realistic, given the staff time available. Then allow yourself at least as much time again for summarising and interpreting the information.

Third, this chapter includes some comments on using computers. It is vital to realise that, although a computer will speed up and simplify a lot of the work described here, it can also create new problems. A computer can have implications including extra cost, staff training and changes in the design of the project. For example, you will need to design survey questionnaires so that data can easily be typed into the computer, in a form which fits the programme you are using. Always plan this ahead — if possible, with the advice of a computer expert.

Checking and correcting raw data

Your first task is to check the quality of the raw data. There will usually be some missing data on several forms. Perhaps the question was never asked; or the respondent was confused or refused to answer. Perhaps the answer is illegible. Much of the checking and correcting of raw data should take place during fieldwork. In Chapter Three, we stressed the need for supervisors to pick out missing data during initial checks. They should discuss this with fieldworkers and note the reasons on the form. But checking goes further than looking for obvious mistakes on individual forms. A debriefing session for the team will bring out problems with the wording of questions or failures to answer.

Also in Chapter Three, we suggested that you design a filing system for completed forms. For example, you can keep a chart showing when forms are returned by fieldworkers, checked and corrected. Another way to avoid data getting lost is to file corrected forms by study area.

Coding

The next stage is to complete coding work for those questions which were not automatically coded in the field. As we saw in Chapter Four, with closed questions this means carefully working through the coding instructions. Whether or not you are using computers, you will be glad of a well-designed form. Clearly identified boxes, with variable numbers next to them, make it easy to pick out the coded information and any missing values.

You will also need to develop a full coding system for any open questions on the form, doing this by hand and using a counting sheet. Work through the forms listing each new answer type as it occurs. Keep count of how many times each answer type is repeated. Place a tally (dash) in the count column each time that answer comes up. (Counting is faster if, when you have four tallies, you place the fifth one across it.) Ask two separate coders to work out a system for each question. There are no firm rules in the development of codes and it is useful to compare different opinions. Give a code to each main answer type and, in addition, give a code to an 'other' category to deal with answers that don't fit the main codes. Include codes for missing data: a 'not applicable' and a 'don't know' code are the most common. (Do not use the 'other' category for missing data, but keep it for answers which are unusual, but meaningful.)

Using data cards and sheets

With a sample size of more than 75 to l00 it can become impractical to work directly with the fieldwork forms. Instead, use data cards or data sheets, unless you are entering data directly on to a computer. Data cards can be filled out by fieldworkers for the forms they complete, using one data card for each respondent. The data is recorded in summary form, as in this example:

Source:	M	l2	01	o4	02	⁄	JAWSS:HHQ		
Quantity:	M	8o	01	2o	02	⁄	No: l26		
Location: Bathing	0/4	ι		Cooking	ι		Storage	ι	
	5/14	ι		Brewing	⁄		Boil	2	
	15+	ι		Clothes	ι		Filter	3	
							Purifier	3	
Supply Problems:	1	⁊	2	⁄	3	⁄			
Time: Queuing	4		All	3		Total Daily Trips	4		
Sickness: Total PC:			0-4	o		Diarrhoea PC :	0-4	o	
			All	4			All	0	
Jobs:	1 3o	2	⁄	4	⁄	Household	0-4	ι	
		3	⁄	5	⁄	Size:	All	8	

The cards can usually be made locally, and are quite cheap. They should be stored in a standard card index box. If you are not using computers, data cards make manual analysis much easier. Simply sort and count the cards to prepare one- and two-way tables.

Data sheets record coded information in a very condensed form. A simple data sheet looks like this:

Form Number	Sex	Age		Household Size		Ethnic Group		
0	1	1	2	0	0	4	0	1
0	2	2	3	4	0	5	0	1
0	3	2	1	4	0	5	0	1
0	4	2	2	2	0	3	0	6
0	5	1	3	4	0	3	0	1
0	6	1	1	2	0	6	0	1
0	7	2	0	8	0	3	0	3
0	8	1	0	2	0	4	0	3
0	9	2	1	6	0	4	0	1

The name of each variable is listed on the sheet in the order in which it appears on the form. Taking each form in turn, codes are transferred to the data sheet. In the example, each form fills a single row. For a very small survey you can enter all the forms onto a single, large data sheet. Mount this on the wall, then use it for data analysis.

Remember that new errors can occur at coding and tabulation stages, so careful checking is vital. You will reduce errors if coders have thorough training and good working conditions, with plenty of rest breaks. A coder should not have to work on the same group of questions day after day. A useful check is to take a regular sample of each coder's output and have it recoded by someone else. Where there is a high level of disagreement, you may need extra training sessions.

Preparing data tables

At the same time as you draft out the fieldwork form, work out a list of the variables you will look at and the tables you want to produce. This is called the tabulation plan, and is the framework on which you will build all your data analysis. (If you are unsure about one-way and two-way tables, please re-read the section on 'Variables and Tables' in Chapter Six.)

In practice, you will develop the tabulation plan in stages. Take one research question at a time and work out all the tables that apply to that question. The plan should never be rigid. You may want to add or remove tables as your understanding of the study questions increases.

Prepare a standard table layout for both one- and two-way tables, and have it duplicated. It should be laid out with:

• Plenty of space.

• Categories for each variable (at least six).

• A percentage column for each variable.

• Spaces to record variable names, the title of the survey, and summary measures (mean and standard deviation, in particular).

If you put one standard data table on each sheet, you can use the space below the table to summarise the most important findings. File completed tables together with the tabulation plan, and a tabulation progress chart to serve as the index.

You will see how the previous coding work prepares the data for your tables. However, in a very small survey, you may not want to use codes. Instead, you can use a counting sheet to prepare a one-way table for each variable. Similarly, if you lay out a counting sheet in boxes corresponding to the combination of variables on each form, you can prepare a two-way table, taking each form in turn, and marking a tally on the sheet, in the corresponding box:

Variable name Rent paid	Variable name Number of rooms rented		
	1	2	3 or more
0 - 9	̶H̶H̶T̶ ̶H̶H̶T̶ ̶H̶H̶T̶	̶H̶H̶T̶ ̶H̶H̶T̶	
10 - 14	̶H̶H̶T̶ ̶H̶H̶T̶ ̶H̶H̶T̶ ̶H̶H̶T̶ ̶H̶H̶T̶		̶H̶H̶T̶
15 - 19	̶H̶H̶T̶ II	̶H̶H̶T̶ ̶H̶H̶T̶ ̶H̶H̶T̶	
20 - 29		̶H̶H̶T̶ ̶H̶H̶T̶ ̶H̶H̶T̶ ̶H̶H̶T̶ ̶H̶H̶T̶	̶H̶H̶T̶ ̶H̶H̶T̶ ̶H̶H̶T̶ ̶H̶H̶T̶ ̶H̶H̶T̶ ̶H̶H̶T̶
30 or more		̶H̶H̶T̶ IIII	̶H̶H̶T̶ ̶H̶H̶T̶ ̶H̶H̶T̶

Preparing tables manually (without a computer) is hard and tedious work. Working from data sheets, a target of l0 to l5 tables per person per day is probably realistic, depending on the sample size. Working directly from fieldwork forms will be even slower.

Use of computers

Where computers are available they can greatly ease many stages of the survey process, from laying out and editing the survey questionnaire, to analysing and presenting the data for your final report. Even a small personal computer has the power to store information from several hundred survey forms together with the programmes you will need to analyse them. A computer reduces the risk of human error and releases time for a more thorough and advanced data analysis.

Usually, you enter coded data directly into the computer, using a keyboard connected to the machine. The computer 'remembers' the data and stores it in an electronic file. It can prepare data tables, draw graphs and calculate statistics in a fraction of the time it takes to do this work by hand. Where a computer is available, or when you are thinking of buying one, get an expert assessment at an early stage of research design, of just how useful it will be to your project. The following outline will help you to ask the right questions.

Choice of computer

The machinery of the computer is called 'hardware'. The hardware components you will need include:

- A computer with keyboard, screen and processor. You will need to be sure that your machine's disc space is large enough to deal with both the survey data and the analysis packages you will be using.

- A printer. Dot matrix printers are good value for money, as they produce text, in a wide variety of fonts, and graphics. They can also be used to produce survey questionnaires.

- Supplies (or 'consumables'). These include extra floppy discs for making spare copies of your data, extra printer ribbons, and paper.

Before choosing a computer for survey work, consider the following:

•Portability. Do you want to type in data and do the initial analysis in the field? If so, it is essential to have portable equipment that is easy and safe to move. Laptop machines are ideal for fieldwork.

•Power supply. Computers need reliable, uninterrupted power. If this is not available, you must either buy a battery-backed 'uninterruptable power supply' (UPS) or use a battery-operated computer which can be recharged using a car battery or solar panel.

•Maintenance and advice. Find out about the local computer market in the area where you plan to do your analysis. (Ask other computer users. They are often a better test of supplier reliability than the suppliers themselves.) If maintenance and advice is available from suppliers of a particular brand of computer, it may be worth getting that brand, even though it is not the cheapest or latest model.

•Planning for a breakdown. Where maintenance and support are not reliable, do not depend on one computer. In this situation it is much wiser to buy two moderately priced computers instead of one expensive one.

Choice of software programmes
To control the computer you need software programmes written in a programming language which your machine understands. While these can be specially written, such full-scale programming is a very specialist skill. Wherever possible, you should rely on standard software packages. An amateur can learn to use these packages over weeks or even days. They are usually better documented and easier to learn than specially-made programme packages that will take extra time and money to develop.
Several types of basic software packages are available including wordprocessing, spreadsheets, databases and statistical analysis packages.

Word processing

Word processing packages turn your computer into an advanced, very flexible typewriter. They are useful for preparing reports, survey forms, and any other documents you need. If you are new to using a computer, choose a wordprocessing package which is widely used in the area where you are doing your survey. You can ask for informal help from other users while you are learning. Some packages offer particularly good facilities for producing graphs and tables in your report. In a country with different script, you may want foreign characters in your report.

Check to see that these programmes are 'compatible' (work) with your other software and your printer.

Database packages

These are useful tools to assist in data entry. You can design a set of standard data entry tables which closely match your questionnaire, so reducing the risk of error. Data can then be exported (copied to) other packages for analysis.

Electronic spreadsheets

These can be used for laying out tables and producing graphs for presenting your data. Data is entered in the spreadsheet in columns and rows, with each row containing a single record, and each column containing a single variable. Spreadsheets provide a flexible system for modifying and analysing your data within this large tabular format. They are useful tools for applying formulae, but are not particularly designed with survey analysis in mind. So an easy-to-use statistical analysis package is likely to be of more value to you for this purpose.

Statistical analysis packages

Good statistical analysis software is a very powerful tool to assist you in all stages of survey data analysis, once the data has been entered in the machine. For example, you can prepare frequency distributions, simple or complex tables, charts and diagrams, in a fully labelled form for inclusion in your final report. Choose a package which is flexible and easy for beginners to use. However, statistical analysis software is not cheap and will take up a fair amount of memory in a personal computer.

As well as these general packages, there are some specially designed survey analysis packages. Within a single package, these cover everything from data-entry and validation (cross-checking) to tabulation and drawing graphs.

Computers in practice

Even with the right machine for the job, together with tried and tested programmes, there remain some important practical points to consider:

• If you are sharing a computer, check that the machine is available when you need it.

• You and your colleagues may need training to use the machine. Do you have the time and other resources for this?

• Errors and delays during programming can occur even with standard software packages. In particular, though data analysis is very fast once your programme is working, you often find many minor difficulties before the programme can be persuaded to work.

Finally, it is vital to remember that you still need to study the computer output and take time over interpretation. A computer cannot replace thoughtful study of the key data.

Making sense of the data

Data interpretation, making sense of the survey results, is by far the most important part of data analysis. This section will suggest how you can use survey data to reach conclusions about each of your research questions. Are your initial ideas confirmed, or do you need to modify them?

As we have stressed, it is more important to use basic statistical tools well, as part of a sensible strategy for data analysis, than to try to use more sophisticated methods. Much of the analysis you need will be simple description of the target population, estimating key variables such as mean household size and median household income. Calculate one-way tables and averages, and convert proportions to percentages (unless the sample size is very small). You may also want to look at the relationship between some of the variables.

Remember that graphs can be used not only to illustrate but to help to analyse data. For example, a scatter diagram can give an indication of the relationship between two numerical variables.

For the research projects referred to in this book, the following questions were asked, to investigate relationships between variables:

HOUSING AREA

$ per month	Informal	%	4th	%	3rd	%	1st/2nd	%
INCOME 0 - 49	16	28	14	12	4	7	1	2
GROUP 50 - 99	18	30	39	34	6	11	0	0
100 -149	10	17	20	17	4	7	1	2
150 -199	7	12	18	16	9	16	6	20
200 -299	5	9	15	13	9	16	3	3
300 -399	1	2	6	5	4	7	7	23
400 -499	1	2	3	3	21	36	12	40
TOTAL	**58**	**100**	**115**	**100**	**57**	**100**	**30**	**100**

- Were households with a higher income more likely to have a pit latrine?

- Was 'type of water source used' related to 'satisfaction with water source'?

- Were building materials used on the plot related to 'length of residence' on the plot?

- Was adults' 'level of education' related to their age or sex?

HOUSING AREA

	Informal	4th Class	3rd Class	1st/2nd Class
Mean Income ($)	108.6	141.0	293.8	326.2
Standard Deviation	90.7	102.6	174.7	146.0

In this example, using the formula on p. 82 ,

$$\text{sample average plus or minus } 2\left(\frac{\text{standard deviation}}{\sqrt{\text{sample size}}}\right)$$

approximate confidence intervals are:

Informal	$85.0 - $132.0
4th Class	$131.0 - $150.6
3rd Class	$270.7 - $316.9
1st/2nd Class	$299.5 - $352.9

98

Always remember that you cannot explore every possible relationship. Look at those which are likely to exist, on the evidence you already have; are relevant to practical problems and to project design; and need to be tested (are not obvious).

Using percentages to compare sub-groups

The two-way table is the basic tool for the study of relationships between variables. Because the sub-groups you are looking at usually have different sample sizes, it is difficult to directly compare distributions within them. In order to do so, it is better to convert the figures into percentages. In the table below, comparing income distributions in different housing areas is easier if you have a percentage column for each area:

Measures of spread
You can also calculate averages and measures of spread for two-way tables. Treat each column, or each row, as a one-way table and calculate the summary measures for each one. For example, the next table summarises data showing income for groups in different housing areas.

Because confidence intervals for the informal and 4th class areas overlap, there is no strong evidence to say that mean income levels differ in these two areas. The same is true for mean income levels in the 3rd and 1st/2nd class areas. There is clear evidence of income differences between informal and 4th class areas, and 3rd and 1st/2nd class areas. (For more exact methods of comparing values for two or more classes, see books listed in Bibliography.)

Three-way tables

Where the sample size is large you may be able to extend analysis to look at the relationship between three variables at once. For example, you may want to examine income levels against latrine ownership in different towns; or you could see whether this relationship changes according to length of residence on the plot.

To answer these questions, use a three-way table. For example, you can group the sample into households resident on their plot for less than 6 months; 6 months to a year; and over one year. Because it is not possible to put all the information into a single table, you will have to prepare three two-way tables showing 'total household income' against 'possession of a latrine' one for each of these three 'length of residence' groups.

Do not assume that wherever you find a relationship between two variables, this is due to cause and effect. Just because more high income households have a latrine, for example, does not mean that lack of income in itself is the main obstacle to latrine ownership. The main problem may be something else; perhaps lack of space on the plot.

In this case, to see whether income and plot-size are important you would need to prepare a three-way table of latrine ownership, against income, for different plot sizes. If income effects latrine ownership in each 'plot-size' group, you know that income does have a direct effect on the decision to build a latrine.

Some final general points

Sometimes you will be able to analyse sub-sets of your data at the same time as you are gathering it. This can help to identify problems at an early stage and allow you to correct them through extra training for fieldworkers or modifying the forms. In addition, where conclusions drawn from the data are of value to the local community, this is an excellent chance to give them immediate feedback.

Remember that the statistical tools you are using are only approximate. They do not take account of inaccuracies due to non-sampling error or the use of over-complicated sample designs. Don't attach too much importance to small differences which will occur between samples, purely by chance. Look for large differences and draw your conclusions from these. Suspend judgement where the sample difference is small.

SUMMARY

The raw data from the survey needs to be checked and processed before it can be used. For a large survey, the use of codes is essential. A coding system allocates numbers to each response or category of response to every question in your survey. Data cards and summary sheets can be used to record codes in summary form.

You should devise a tabulation plan, listing the tables and charts you want to produce from your data. Where computers are available, they can speed up the processing of survey data, using standard software packages.

Remember that the interpretation of the results is the most important part of data analysis. Consider how best to analyse the data to answer your research questions.

8 PRESENTING THE FINDINGS

How will you effectively communicate the findings of your research — especially to people with power to act on the information? You and your colleagues may have spent months finding out and analysing important data. But that time and effort, on their own, do not guarantee that others will hear about your work. While there are no simple answers, some general guidelines will help.

One essential point is to think about the full range of audiences you want to reach. You will usually need separate approaches for different groups such as aid agency staff, technicians, professionals, government officials and community members. This chapter begins with advice on writing up your findings, using tables and diagrams to clarify and emphasise what you need to say. But, though a good report is a basic starting point, it is not the end of your work. You need to consider other methods as part of a wider communication strategy. For example, giving a talk is often the most effective way of getting your message across. Then there are other tools: drawings and photography; video and tape/slide presentation and drama. You might also consider the use of public information media such as newspapers and radio.

Planning a report

Plan the report structure carefully. A report of findings should tell the reader how and why the research was done; what you learnt about the study problems; and what you think should be done to improve the situation.

These three broad questions are answered in the corresponding three parts of the report:

- Introduction,

- Presentation and Analysis of Data, and

- Conclusions and Recommendations.

The introduction
Work through the following checklist, giving your reader brief information on each of these topics:

- why the research was done,

- when the research was done,

- who conducted the research,

- who paid,

- what information was collected,

- what methods were used to choose the sample,

- what practical problems were met during fieldwork,

- how reliable the results are.

Make sure you list the subjects on which you asked questions. Many people choose to include the research questionnaire as an appendix to their report.

The description of methods can be brief. Knowing when to stop is a virtue in any report writer. But give the reader enough detail to decide how widely the results can be used. For example, it is not enough just to give a sample size. You must also say how you chose that sample.

If the study is a case study, say so. Usually you will name the villages, housing areas, or locations in which the fieldwork was conducted. But always be careful to respect promises of confidentiality given to respondents.

Briefly explain the major fieldwork problems. Indicate how many people refused to co-operate, or could not be contacted. If

103

circumstances forced you to modify the sampling method, describe any modifications. Try to give a general picture of the reliability of the results.

Presentation and analysis of data

The presentation and analysis is the heart of a report. Plan it thoroughly before you begin writing. Start by making an outline structure based on the research questions. Use these to work out headings and sub-headings. Now list the main points for every sub-section, which can each become one paragraph. In general, make your main point as the first sentence of each paragraph.

Think about other information you may want to put in. Is there useful case-study material? Can you illustrate some points effectively with quotations from answers recorded in the field? You may want to compare results with earlier research or studies from elsewhere. Choose exactly what you want to include before you start writing. Look at the data tables you are going to use, and decide which tables belong in which sub-section. If you have not already done so, decide which points you want to make from each table. If there are no points of interest in a particular table, why are you including it? Use data tables, or diagrams based on them, to present the detailed survey results. The written text will then explain what the results mean. Don't repeat the contents of tables or diagrams in written form. Instead, focus the reader's attention on the important results and relate those results to the problem under discussion. Consider the next example. How would you improve it?

There is an extreme shortage of sanitation facilities in Juba. As indicated in Table A (Sanitation Facilities in Juba), only about 20 per cent of households have a latrine in working order. Table A also illustrates the situation in different types of housing area. Only first and second class areas, together comprising about 6 per cent of the population of Juba, are fully serviced with latrines. In the third class areas, comprising 7 per cent of the population, about 80 per cent of households have a latrine. The situation is far worse in the fourth class areas, where less than 15 per cent have a latrine, and in the informal areas, where the proportion is about 5 per cent. 50 per cent of the population are living in fourth class areas and 30 per cent in informal areas. (Juba Urban Area Sanitation Survey, 1982)

Table A : Sanitation Facilities in Juba

Housing Area	Complete Latrines	
	N	%
Informal	68	6
4th class	135	13
3rd class	78	78
1st/2nd class	37	100
Juba Urban Area	318	19

N = Size of sample   (JUASS 1982)

The example illustrates some good features. The paragraph begins with a main point and then directs the reader's attention to the evidence backing up that point (and nothing else). It also says what the data table means. Because the figures in the text are 'rounded off' to the nearest 5 per cent, they are easier to digest. The main weakness is that there are too many figures in the text. Most figures are given in detail in the data table; there is no need to repeat them. The total population breakdown by housing class is very important, so it would be better to include this as a separate table in the report, then the exact figures need not be given in the text. We can rewrite the paragraph like this:

There is an extreme shortage of sanitation facilities in Juba. Only about 20 per cent (one fifth) of households have a latrine in working order (see Table A). Most households in first, second and third class areas have a latrine. But most of the population lives in fourth class and informal areas, where few households have a complete latrine. The situation is worst in informal areas, where only about one household in twenty has a latrine. The detailed sample breakdown is given in Table A..

This makes the same points as the original, but is easier to read. The most important percentage in the table is given in the text, in rounded form. A reader who wants detailed information on one housing class looks up the data table. Notice how this table is referred to in the text.

Conclusions and recommendations

Give plenty of time for thinking over and developing good conclusions and recommendations. Discuss your ideas as widely as possible before you finalise them. Make sure they are clear, practical and realistic in the light of available resources. Keep two points in mind. First, most readers will judge the value of the research by the quality of the conclusions and recommendations. Second, people can expect, and sometimes demand, too precise and reliable conclusions, particularly from surveys. The report writer has a responsibility for avoiding unsupported claims. Even so, a conclusion is more than just a summary of findings — it is a point of view or opinion based on the research findings. For example:

80 per cent of households in Juba have no latrine, but most of these households regard the lack of adequate sanitation facilities as a very serious problem.

The survey did not prove this. It did not even ask, directly, whether people saw a lack of sanitation facilities as a serious problem. The relevant findings from the survey were:

•Of those households without a latrine, 25 per cent have tried to build one.

•Most partly built latrines are at least three metres deep.

•Of those households without a complete or partly-built latrine, 20 per cent have plans to build one during the next twelve months.

These findings were enough to convince the researchers that many households do, in fact, see sanitation as a serious problem. However, when writing a report it is important to make a clear distinction between reporting on the findings of the survey and when you are moving beyond these and drawing conclusions from them. Having reached a conclusion: what should be done about it? A recommendation goes further, pointing to a plan of action. In the example above, the recommendation was that:

There is an important role for technical advice and extension work to ensure that the existing self-help construction is encouraged and directed using appropriate low-cost designs.

This is a very general recommendation. It is a starting point for discussion with the government units and agencies involved. More specific recommendations can only be made after these discussions take place.

The summary

A report of more than one or two pages must have a summary. Put the summary at the front. To help the reader refer from the summary to the main report, use the same system of headings and sub-headings in both. Remember that many readers will only read the summary. So make it self-contained, apart from references to the data tables. For the same reason, the most important bit of the summary will be the conclusions and recommendations. As part of your overall communication strategy, think about using the summary as a separate document. With a few key tables added, would it make an effective two- or four-page pamphlet?

Listing sources and references

If you use someone else's work in a report you must refer to it. This is to give them credit, and to enable readers to read it for themselves. Use abbreviations to avoid cluttering the text with detailed references — for example: (Nichols 1990). List your full sources at the end, arranged in alphabetical order by author. The usual convention is to give the title, publisher and date of publication. However, remember that the majority of potential readers may not have access to a good library. You should consider adding a contact address where readers can get hold of the publication.

Spacing and headings

Normally use one and a half space typing. When you want to circulate a draft, use double spacing, so readers can write notes. Work out a structure for the different types of heading and stick to it. Three types of heading should be enough for most reports. The structure used in this handbook is:

CHAPTER TITLE

Main heading

Sub-heading

Language and style

We have looked at planning a logical structure for the report. Now we will discuss the use of language — something just as vital in achieving clear communication. Reports are easier to read when written in a straightforward language and style. The following suggestions will help you to write good, plain English:

•Know what you want to say. Decide what needs saying before you start to write. Then say it as simply as possible.

•Avoid jargon and difficult words. Use words that your readers will understand and always explain words that may be new to them. Define essential technical terms in the text, putting the rest in a glossary at the end.

•Avoid long and complicated sentences. You do not want your readers to get lost. Several short sentences are usually clearer than one long one. Sometimes it helps to give lists of items or conditions in a step-by-step form.

•Use the space you need. Ease of reading and understanding is more important than reducing the volume of writing.

•Choose 'active' sentences. For example, instead of: 'The rock problem was mentioned by most households', write: 'Most households mentioned the rock problem'. Though some academic writers prefer the more complicated passive form, avoid it unless you want to focus attention on the object.

•Don't use brackets or commas to cram ideas together. For example, avoid something like this:

Improved maize production, which is one of the primary community concerns (based on the district survey), was the topic of the meeting.

Instead, put separate main ideas into a fresh sentence:

Improved maize production was the topic of the meeting. The district survey found it to be one of the primary concerns of the community.

•Avoid complicated tenses. Use the simple present, past or future whenever possible.

•Give the meaning of abbreviations and colloquial words. Use abbreviations as little as possible. Make sure you give the meaning the first time you use any abbreviation, and from time to time to refresh the reader's memory. Colloquial words are those which are used only in one area, or in a special way. For example: 'Most people collect water by the 'tin' (an 18 litre plastic or metal container)'.

•Use simple link words. A link word signals the direction in which the argument is moving. For example: 'The situation is better among upper income families. Even so, most have no latrine'. Choose simple link words such as: also; even so; on the other hand; in the same way. Avoid more complicated words like: moreover; nevertheless; notwithstanding.

To sum up, edit your work to make it clear and readable. Look at your words and sentences. Have you chosen straightforward language and avoided unnecessary words? Is there a simpler way of saying the same thing? If there is, use it. Finally, there is one sure method for improving a piece of writing. If your colleagues can bear it, read the draft out loud!

Presenting numbers
The mind can only digest a few numbers at a time. So the best place for detailed numbers is in data tables or diagrams. Use the written text to pick out the most important numbers and say what they mean. Surveys produce estimates, not the exact truth. It is usually best to round percentages to the nearest whole number. In the text, additional rounding up reminds the reader that the sample value is only an estimate. For example, not '19 per cent', but 'about 20 per cent'. To help a non-technical audience, 'about 20 per cent' can be written as 'about one in five'.

Laying out tables
Every table must have:

•a title,

•a table number,

•a reference to the source of information,

• a reference to the sample size,

• a full description of what each figure refers to.

For example:

Pit Latrines: Actual costs and estimated costs
n=288

Cost	% of households with a complete latrine (Actual Costs)	% of households with a partly-built latrine (Estimated total cost)	% of households with no latrine Estimated (Estimated total cost)
	N=41	N=71	N=176
Less than $100	30	10	0
$100 to $499	35	40	47
$500 or more	35	50	53

Source: JUASS (Juba Area Sanitation Survey) 1982

In a two-way table like this, you must give the sample size for each column (or row). Note that the usual abbreviation for sample size is the letter 'N' (or 'n'). Explain this in a footnote in the first table in the report.

Diagrams and pictures

Diagrams and pictures are powerful tools for use in reports, presentations and workshops. Especially for readers who are nervous of numbers, they can present quantitative data with great clarity. All diagrams and pictures must have:

• a title,

• a reference to the source of the information,

• a reference to the sample size.

In Chapter Six we looked at most of the common types of diagrams: bar chart; histogram; and scatter diagram. Look again at those examples, this time thinking how you could illustrate the data in your own report.

Which will best attract attention to key data, and show overall patterns? The pie chart is another commonly used diagram. It is an effective way of showing proportions at a glance. In a sample, each sub-group is drawn as one segment of a circle ('a slice of the pie') in proportion to its size. Variations of the pie chart can emphasise different aspects.

Pictures and illustrations

Pictures and illustrations help to make a report lively and interesting. They are often more effective than written text for communicating straightforward messages. When reading skills are low, they are essential.

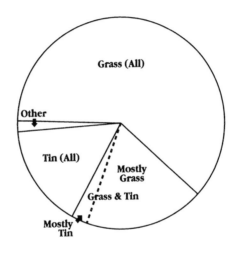

Pie Chart: Roof Materials

To calculate the size of each slice;

Roof Materials	%	Degrees (%x 3.6)
Grass all	63	227˚
Grass and tin, mostly grass	17	61˚
Grass and tin, mostly tin	7	25˚
Tin mostly	12	43˚
Other (mostly tile)	1	4˚
	100	360

But even highly educated audiences prefer some clear graphics, rather than just large blocks of unbroken print. Pictorial methods, like written material, should match your audience. Pamphlets or small posters are ideal for simple, key ideas. For a more technical audience, pictorial graphs are useful.

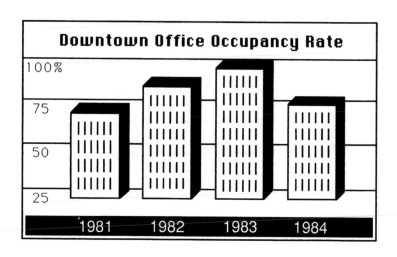

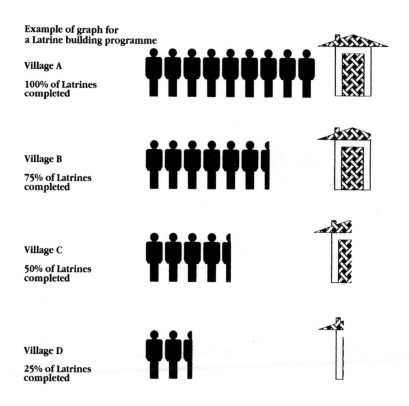

Example of graph for a Latrine building programme

Village A

100% of Latrines completed

Village B

75% of Latrines completed

Village C

50% of Latrines completed

Village D

25% of Latrines completed

112

**An example of
a finance graph**

EDUCATION WORK

COSTS

WORKING CAPITAL

ADMINISTRATION

82p 11p 4p 3p

**Example of graph for
Resources – Who consumes most?**

The Developing world has...

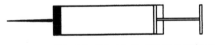

6% of the Worlds Health Expenditure

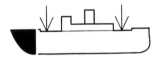

18% of the World Export Earnings

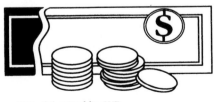

17% of the World's GNP

30% of the Food Grains

But illustrations are not always a reliable means of communication. It is essential to pre-test them with members of the target audience to make sure they understand what you intend. For instance, are they familiar with graphics conventions such as cutaway drawings, and plans? Similarly, a 'comic-strip' format will only work if your audience knows its conventions — like speech 'balloons'. When your illustrations show people, try to portray your readers' own recognisable social world, with typical styles of dress, and scenery. If you have no colleagues easily available with the necessary graphic skills, check if some local artists can help. Or look at some of the books of illustrations, published especially for development settings. These collections — called 'imagebanks' — have been tried and tested by local projects. As the artists have given up their copyright, you can use and adapt them to your own setting.

Using other communication tools

A face-to-face meeting is often the best way to communicate. You can feed information directly to project management meetings and similar technical groups. Organise seminars and workshops for other agencies and community groups. Sometimes you may be able to make a live presentation before you finish your final report. You can learn from such discussions to improve your proposals and recommendations.

Plan each spoken presentation carefully, tailoring the material to suit your audience. Prepare and duplicate a checklist of main points, in addition to the more detailed summary of findings. Structure your presentation around the checklist. For community groups and non-technical audiences keep your style very straightforward. Present key findings as simply as possible, aiming above all to stimulate discussion. Avoid long presentations and don't use complicated diagrams or tables.

Get feedback on the survey results. Does the group think they make sense? What should be done about them? Do they feel that the study got to the bottom of the problems?

A short tape-slide presentation is often a useful tool. Build up a sequence of photos taken in the study area, including detailed shots of particular problems. To include maps or diagrams, first prepare the illustration to a large, display size, then photograph it from close range. A presentation of ten to fifteen minutes is usually about right, including thirty or more slides — aim to show each slide for about fifteen to twenty seconds. Keep the spoken commentary simple and fairly slow. It should be much easier to follow than written material. The aim is to

114

generate interest and discussion, using themes picked out from the study. Do not try to cover all the ground; instead, concentrate on the main points, keeping figures to a minimum.

Rather than always basing a live presentation on the structure of your report, it is often simpler to focus on conditions for a case-study family or village. You can prepare alternative versions of the commentary for different audiences. Translations can include local languages and dialects as appropriate.

Drama is sometimes a useful method for live presentations to community groups. A play can illustrate typical situations, again developing themes from the study. Done well, this arouses immediate interest and can lead directly into a discussion of research. You can also develop simple themes for a comic strip series. In both cases you will need to work closely with specialists. Prepare them a very clear brief, summarising the themes and material.

Another option is to get press or radio coverage. A press release can raise interest, and you can try to fit the timing with other events, such as presentations. However, always remember that, as your research findings begin to enter the 'public arena', there may be dangers. For example, news items which exaggerate or raise false hopes will do more harm than good. Discuss these risks with your colleagues and other local partners. Can you get co-operation from local journalists in avoiding misleading publicity?

SUMMARY

Having carried out a survey and analysed the data, the final stage is to present your findings to the various people and groups you want to communicate with.

A written report is essential and this should be well-planned and clearly and simply written. A report will begin by describing how the survey was carried out, will probably include tables and other summaries of the survey findings and finish by listing your conclusions and recommendations.

You might also want to give talks and other presentations. These should be carefully designed to suit the needs and interests of the particular audience. Visual aids — charts, slides, illustrations — are helpful. Other means of communicating such as drama, comic strips, radio or press coverage, may also be appropriate.

BIBLIOGRAPHY

Board of Science and Technology for International Development (BOSTID), (1988), *Cutting Edge Technologies and Microcomputer Applications for Developing Countries,* London: Intermediate Technology Publications/Westview.

Bulmer, M. and Warwick, D.D. (eds) (1983), *Social Research in Developing Countries: Surveys and Censuses in the Third World,* London: Wiley.

Casley, D.J. and Lury, D.A. (1981), *Data Collection in Developing Countries,* Oxford: Clarendon Press.

Cochran, W.G. (1977), *Sampling Techniques,* London: Sage.

Coleman, G. (1982), *Labour Data Collection in African Traditional Agricultural Systems,* University of East Anglia, Development Studies Occasional Paper, Norwich: University of East Anglia.

Connell, J. and Lipton, M. (1977), *Assessing Village Labour Situations in Developing Countries,* Delhi, India: Oxford University Press.

Devine, F. (1982), *Basic Statistics,* London: Harrap.

Feuerstein, M.T. (1986), *Partners in Evaluation,* London: Macmillan.

Fink, A. and Kosecoff, J. (1985), *How to Conduct Surveys: A Step by Step Guide,* Beverley Hills, USA: Sage.

Gardner, G. (1978), *Social Surveys for Social Planners,* Milton Keynes: Open University Press.

Hoinville, G. and Jowell, R. (1978), *Survey Research Practice*, London: Heinemann Educational Books.

Idaikkador, N.M. (1979), *Agricultural Statistics : a Handbook for Developing Countries*, Oxford: Pergamon.

Lipton, M. and Moore, M. (1972), *The Methodology of Village Studies in Less Developed Countries*, Institute of Development Studies Discussion Paper No. 10, Brighton: University of Sussex.

Moser, C.A. and Kalton, G. (1979), *Survey Methods in Social Investigation*, London: Heinemann Educational Books.

Peil M. et al, (1982) *Social Science Research Methods : an African Handbook*, London: Hodder and Stoughton.

Pratt, B. (forthcoming), *Data Collection for Fieldworkers, Development Guidelines Series*, Oxford: Oxfam.

Rowntree, D. (1981), *Statistics without Tears: A Primer for Non-mathematicians*, London: Penguin.

Sethuraman, S.V. (ed) (1981), *The Urban Informal Sector in Developing Countries: Employment, Poverty and Environment*, Geneva, Switzerland: International Labour Organisation.

Simpson-Herbert, M. (1983), *Methods for Gathering Socio-Cultural Data for Water Supply and Sanitation Projects*, Technical Note No. 1, Washington, USA: IBRD/World Bank.

UNICEF (1978), *Keep Your Village Clean: a Handbook for Community Workers*, New York, USA: UNICEF.

World Health Organisation (1977), *Rapid Village Nutrition Survey Technique*, Geneva, Switzerland: WHO.

GLOSSARY

active (mode):
Sentences in the form subject-verb-object, for example 'He dug the hole'. Sentences in the form object-verb, for example 'The hole was dug', are termed passive.

answer list:
A standard range of possible answers which the interviewers read out to the respondent. Respondents choose which answer(s) they agree with.

attitude scale:
A list of attitude statements, arranged in order, which the interviewer reads out loud. Respondents select the statement which they agree with.

average:
A measure of the centre of a distribution.

axis:
Straight line measuring distance in a single dimension. Used of graphs.

back-translation:
A technique for checking the translation of questionnaires. One person translates the original into the required language. A second person translates the translation back into the original language.

base variable:
To convert a two-way table into percentage form, you must first choose a base variable. Within each category of the base variable, percentages must sum to 100.

bias:
Repeated, systematic error. Bias in sampling, for example, means ignoring or under-representing some parts of the target population.

call-back:
Repeat attempt to contact a sample household in a social survey.

case-study:
Study based on a small number of 'typical' examples. Results are not statistically reliable.

chain sample:
See sample.

closed question:
(*See also open question*). The full range of possible answers is listed in advance. The interviewer marks the answer given in each case.

cluster sample:
See sample.

code:
System for summarising information collected in surveys. Each possible answer is given a code (usually a number). Each person's answer is then categorised using the appropriate code for each answer given.

coding instructions:
A full listing of all possible codes, together with the answers they summarise, for each question.

coding sheet:
A sheet recording the coded answers from many respondents. The codes for each respondent are usually recorded along a single row (or column).

communication strategy:
A plan to communicate survey findings. This can include the use of reports, pamphlets, presentations, workshops, tape-slide shows, drama and newspaper or radio coverage.

computer:
Electronic device to store and analyse data.

confidence interval:
Range of values which you can confidently expect will contain the true target population value you are trying to estimate. The confidence limits are the lower and upper values in the confidence interval.

control (group):
A 'standard' group for use in comparisons. You can compare a project area with a 'control' village, for example; this is a village which is similar in many ways to the project area, but without the project of interest.

correlation:
The strength of relationship between two (or more) variables. Positive correlation means that one variable tends to increase together with another variable. Negative correlation means that one variable decreases as the other one increases. The strength of a correlation is measured using values between -1 and >1. A score of zero means there is no relationship.

counting sheet:
A sheet for counting the number of responses in each possible category. A tally is used to record each response in the appropriate position.

coverage rate:
The proportion of the selected sample successfully contacted during fieldwork (usually given as a percentage).

cross-tabulation:
See *two-way table.*

cumulative frequency:
(*See also distribution.*) A count of the number of distribution cases less than a given range of values. For example, a cumulative income distribution may count the number of values less than $50, the number less than $100, the number less than $150, and so on.

data:
Information. The term 'data' often describes information stored in numerical form. Hard data is precise, numerical information. Soft data is less precise, verbal information. Raw data is the name given to survey information before it has been processed and analysed. Missing data are values or responses which fieldworkers were unable to collect (or which were lost before analysis).

data base:
System for storing data in an organised way. The aim is to give future users easy access to available data.

data cards:
Cards on which responses from a single questionnaire are written in summary form.

data processing:
Converting raw data into a usable, meaningful form.

data sheets:
Large sheets of paper on which responses from many questionnaires are recorded in a summary form. Usually, responses from each questionnaire are recorded in a single row (or column).

debriefing:
Discussion with the fieldwork team when fieldwork is complete.

demography:
The study of populations, especially statistics of birth, fertility and death.

deviation:
(*See also* **standard deviation.**) The size of the difference between two numbers. A common measure is deviation from the mean.

distribution:
The full set of sample or population values. A frequency distribution is a table which shows how many times each particular value or item occurs in the sample data.

economic:
Relating to work, income, spending or business.

economic activity:
Work to earn money, whether formal or informal, large-scale or small-scale. This includes small-scale agriculture and work in the home to earn money (such as brewing or baking for sale).

editing:
'Cleaning up' raw data. Checking for mistakes, correcting them where possible, dealing with missing data and creating new variables, as appropriate.

eligible:
Suitable for inclusion in the sample: a member of the target population.

error:
Variation between sample data and the full target population. Error can be systematic (*see* **bias**), or random. Random error is a result of chance differences from sample to sample. Systematic error (bias) occurs where there is a fault in the way the sample is chosen.

evaluation:
Review to assess whether a project has met its objectives. To perform a thorough evaluation, project monitoring is essential.

event calendar:
List of well-known local, regional or national events used to help pin down dates of birth, or other personal events of interest.

experiment:
Carefully designed trial or test, controlling the effect of outside factors. Used in agriculture, for example, to test alternative seed or crop types in controlled conditions.

fertility:
Number of births for each woman. Usually expressed as number of births to a fixed number of women over a fixed time period; per 1000 women per year, for example.

filter:
Form design system to ensure a question, or group of questions, is only put to a particular sub-group in the sample. A preliminary question 'filters' out those who do not apply.

frequency distribution:
See *distribution.*

formal methods:
(*See also* *informal methods*.) Structured research methods, usually using structured interview forms with large samples.

genealogy-based sample:
See *sample.*

guessed mean:
See *mean.*

hard data:
See *data.*

horizontal axis:
See *axis.*

infant mortality:
Number of babies dying before their first birthday out of a fixed number of live births (usually 1000).

informal methods:
(*See also formal methods*.) Less structured, exploratory research methods, such as case-studies or participant-observation.

interquartile range:
A measure of spread. The difference between the upper and lower quartile (*see* *percentile*).

key-informant:
Person carefully chosen for interview because of their special knowledge of some aspect of the target population.

key-words:

Summary question on interview form. The fieldworker is free to decide on exact wording during the interview.

malnutrition:

See *nutrition.*

matched sample:

See *sample.*

mean:

A kind of average for interval variables. Total of the sample values divided by the number of values in the sample. You can use a guessed mean (a round number, close to the true mean) to simplify calculation of the standard deviation.

median:

A kind of average for interval variables. The middle value when the data are arranged in order of size. Where the set of data has an even number of values the median is the mean of the two middle values.

memory:

Power of a computer to store data and programmes.

missing data:

See *data.*

monitoring:

Regular, systematic information collection to assess progress in meeting project objectives.

non-contact:

Member of the sample which the fieldworkers are unable to contact.

non-random sampling:

See *sample.*

non-sampling error:

Error due to factors other than random variation from sample to sample. Non-contacts, refusals, interviewer error, poor form design and errors in data processing all contribute to non-sampling error.

nutrition:
Feeding habits. Science of food, nourishment and health. Malnutrition is poor nutrition.

one-shot survey:
Survey at a single point in time, in contrast to a repeat survey.

one-way table:
See *table*.

open question:
(*See also* *closed question.*) A question to which there can be many different answers. The interviewer writes down the answer in full, using the respondent's own words.

over-sample:
Used in stratified sampling. Instead of fixing the sample size in each strata according to its share of the total population, a larger sample is drawn from those strata with a small total population.

panel survey:
Survey involving several repeat visits to the same fixed sample over a long time period. Useful to study or monitor change over time.

participant observation:
An informal research method. The fieldworker lives and works among the target population for a period of several weeks or months, completing a systematic programme of observation and interview.

percentage:
The proportion (or fraction) in a particular class or sub-group, multiplied by 100.

percentile:
The value in the sample below which a given percentage of the values lie: for example, the 60th percentile has 60% of the sample values below it. The median is the 50th percentile. The upper

125

quartile is the 75th percentile. The lower quartile is the 25th percentile.

personal computer:
A small, desk-top computer designed for use in a small office or business.

pilot survey:
Also known as a pre-test. A small survey, in advance of the main fieldwork, to test the form, sampling procedures and fieldwork management procedures.

pre-test:
See *pilot survey.*

primary sampling unit:
Used in two-stage sampling. Clusters selected in the first stage are called primary sampling units.

probe:
A neutral phrase to encourage respondents to expand on their answer.

programme:
A detailed list of instructions to control the operation of a computer, written in a special programming language. A programme-package contains a wide range of ready-made programmes for use by the non-specialist. Examples of programming languages are BASIC, FORTRAN and PASCAL.

purposive sample:
See *sample.*

questionnaire:
A standard form used by the fieldworker to record a survey interview.

quota sample:
See *sample.*

random error:
See error.

random sampling:
See sample.

random walk:
Fieldworkers follow a carefully pre-set route, interviewing households at regular intervals.

range:
Difference between the highest and lowest value in a set of data.

raw data:
See data.

refusal:
A member of the sample who refuses to be interviewed.

regression:
A statistical technique for studying the strength of relationship between two interval variables.

repeat survey:
Study involving repeated fieldwork over a period of time, rather than a one-shot survey.

respondent:
Person being interviewed.

response rate:
Proportion (or fraction) of the sample who are successfully interviewed.

robust:
Affected little by small changes in the sample values (usually applied to summary measures, such as averages).

rotating survey:

Repeat visits are made to a panel, but on each new visit a fraction of the panel is replaced.

sample:

A selection of units chosen to represent the target population. In random sampling, the method of selection is based on chance and all units in the target population have a known change of begin selected. In non-random sampling the method of selection is based at least partly on the judgement of the researcher or interviewer.

Types of random sampling include: the simple random sample (selection of units by chance in its purest, simplest form);the systematic sample (choose a random point on the list or map and select units spaced at regular intervals from then on); the stratified random sample (use existing information to divide the sample into sub-groups called strata, then select a random sample within each sub-group); the cluster sample (to save time and money, choose the sample from several randomly selected clusters or areas of concentration rather than from the full target population); the two-stage sample (choose a random sample of units from each randomly selected cluster).

Types of non-random sampling include: the purposive sample (selecting units which you believe to be 'typical'); the quota sample (fieldworkers look for an agreed number of people or units of various 'types'); the random walk (fieldworkers follow a pre-set route, interviewing households at regular intervals); the genealogy-based sample (sample entire families, including all close relatives, to get a cross-section of the community); the chain sample (if you are looking for rare or minority units you can sometimes use a first contact to identify further respondents); the matched sample (choose pairs of units which you judge to be 'alike' in some way, for a comparative study).

sampling frame:

A list or map of all the units in the target population.

simple random sample:

See *sample.*

skip:
Instruction to fieldworker to by-pass one or more questions on the form. The by-passed questions are only asked to a particular sub-group in the sample.

social survey:
Fieldworkers use a specially designed form to collect a standard set of information from members of the target population.

soft data:
See *data.*

spread:
Measures of spread tell you how spread out (dispersed) a set of values is. Spread is measured from the centre (middle) of a distribution.

square:
To square a number, multiply it by itself.

square root:
The square root of a number B is the number A which, when squared, will give B. For example, 7 is the square root of 49.

standard deviation:
(*See also* **deviation.**) The mean of squared deviation from the mean is called the variance. The standard deviation is the square root of the variance.

statistical function:
On an electronic calculator, a function is the power to complete a certain type of operation. Addition, multiplication, taking the square root and squaring are examples of possible functions. Statistical functions, included on some calculators, will add up values as you input them and compute their mean and standard deviation.

strata, stratify:
See *sample.*

stratified random sample:
See sample.

structured interview survey:
(*See also* **unstructured interview survey.**) A type of social survey. The range of possible answers to each question is known in advance. Often, possible answers are listed on the form so that the interviewer simply marks the appropriate reply in each case.

sub-sample:
A sample within a sample. For example you can draw a random sub-sample of completed forms to check the quality of fieldwork.

systematic error:
See error and bias.

systematic sampling:
See sample.

table:
A table presents a division of the sample into sub-groups. A one-way table uses the classes of a single variable to define the sub-groups. A two-way table uses the classes of a second variable to further sub-divide each class in the one-way table. A three-way table is actually a series of tables with a separate two-way table for sample values falling into each class of a third variable.

tabulation plan:
List of tables you plan to prepare.

tally:
Method of counting sample values by hand. Before you begin, lay out a table framework with a large box for each sub-group in the table. Work through the forms, marking each response in the appropriate box with a tally - a dash or mark. For easy counting, write the tallies in groups of five like this:

target population:
The full group of people or units of interest.

three-way table:
   See table.

two stage sample:
   See sample.

two-way table:
   See table.

unstructured interview survey:
   (*See also structured interview survey.*) A type of social survey. An informal interview, not structured by a standard list of questions. Fieldworkers are free to deal with the topics of interest in any order and to phrase the questions as they think best.

variable:
   A single characteristic of the target population, such as household size, household income, spending priorities.

variance:
   See standard deviation.

vertical axis:
   See axis.

weight:
   Where you have over-sampled some strata, you need to use weights when you combine results from separate strata to give an estimate for the full target population. Divide the total for each stratum by the sample size in that stratum, then multiply by the proportion (fraction) of the target population in that stratum before adding up the strata results.

work status:
   Worker 'types' such as self-employed, work for a wage or salary, unpaid family worker, or unpaid non-family worker.